Pattern Coloring Books for Adults Relaxation

by Linn Littlebelle

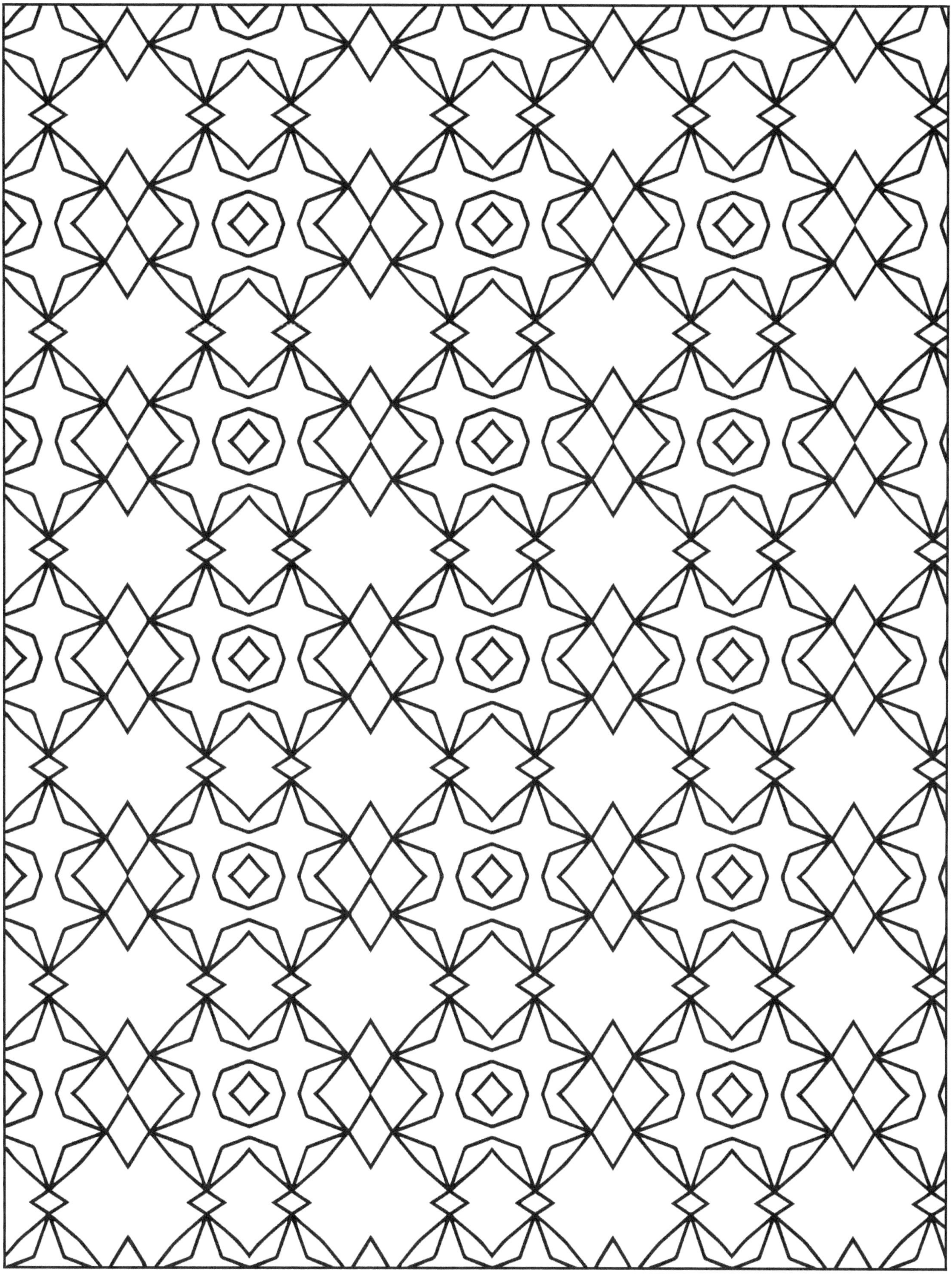

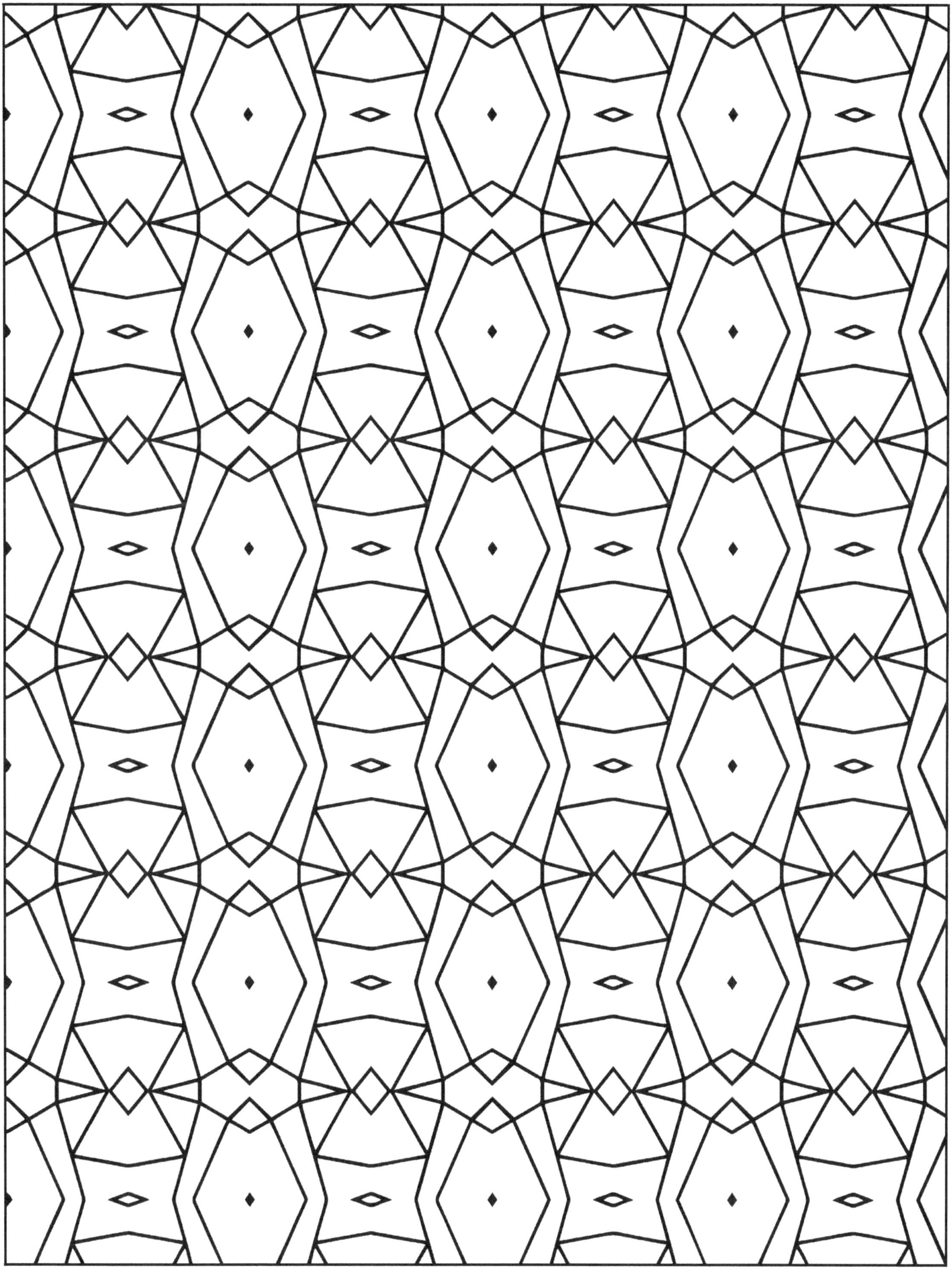

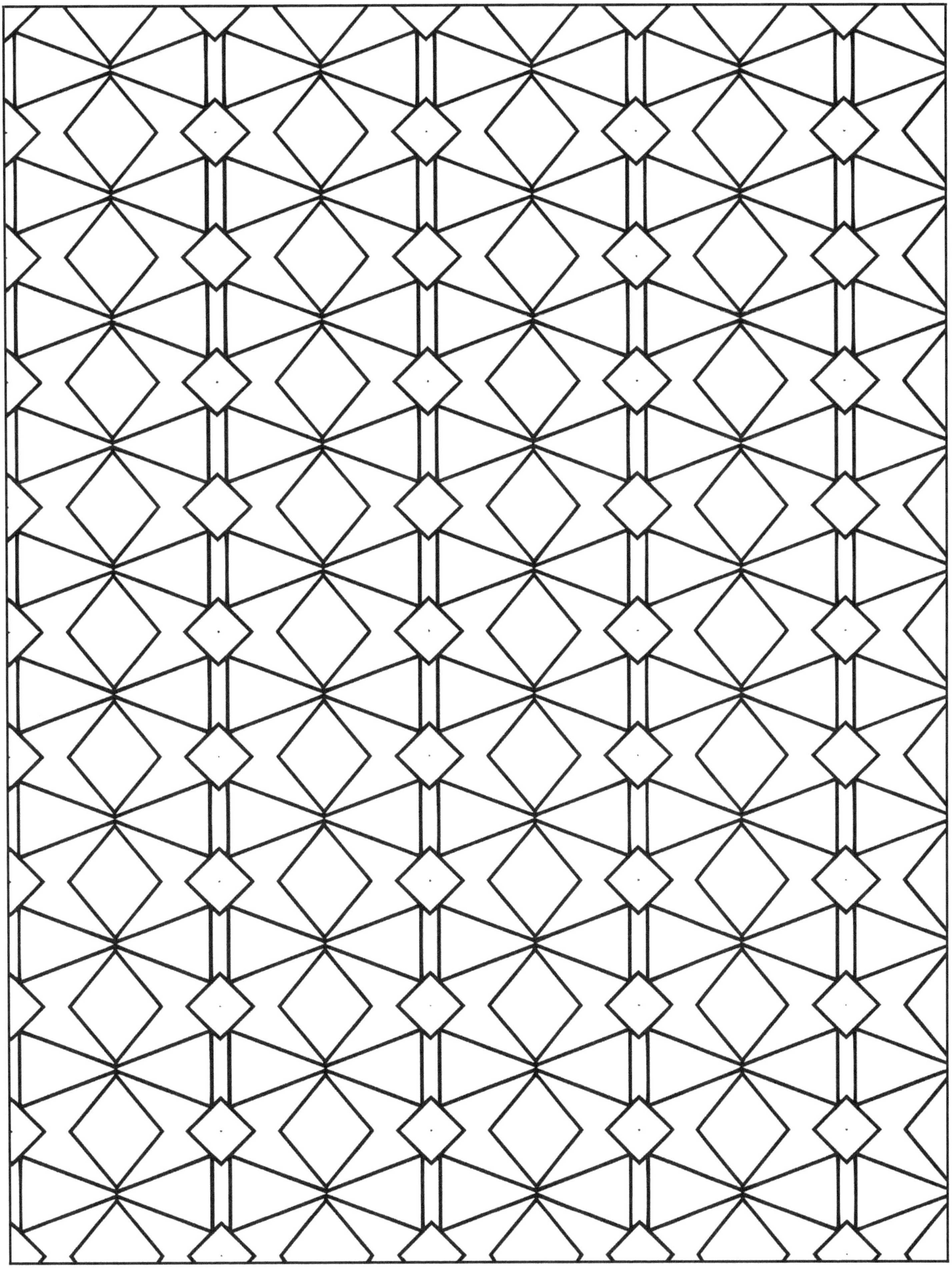

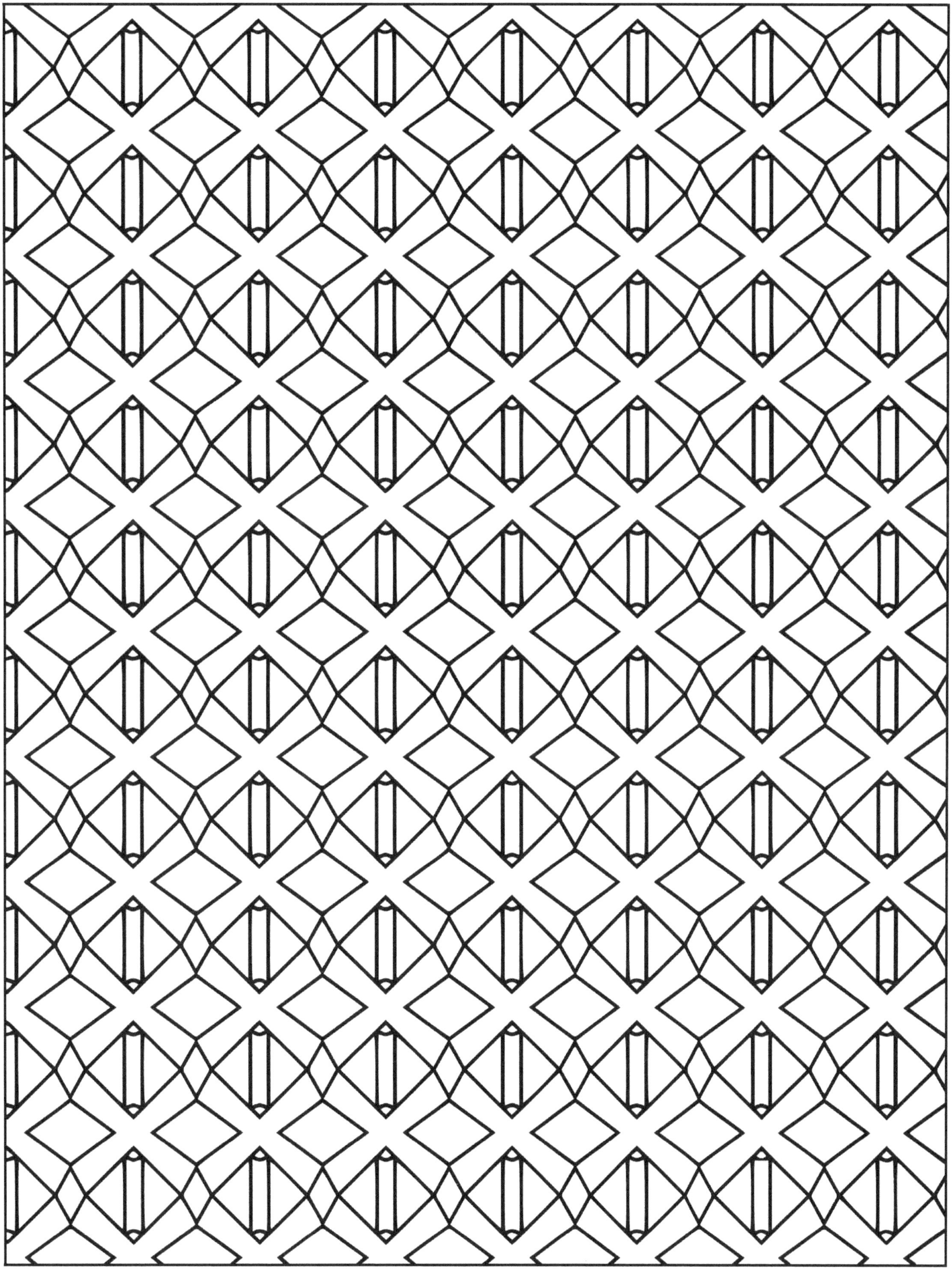

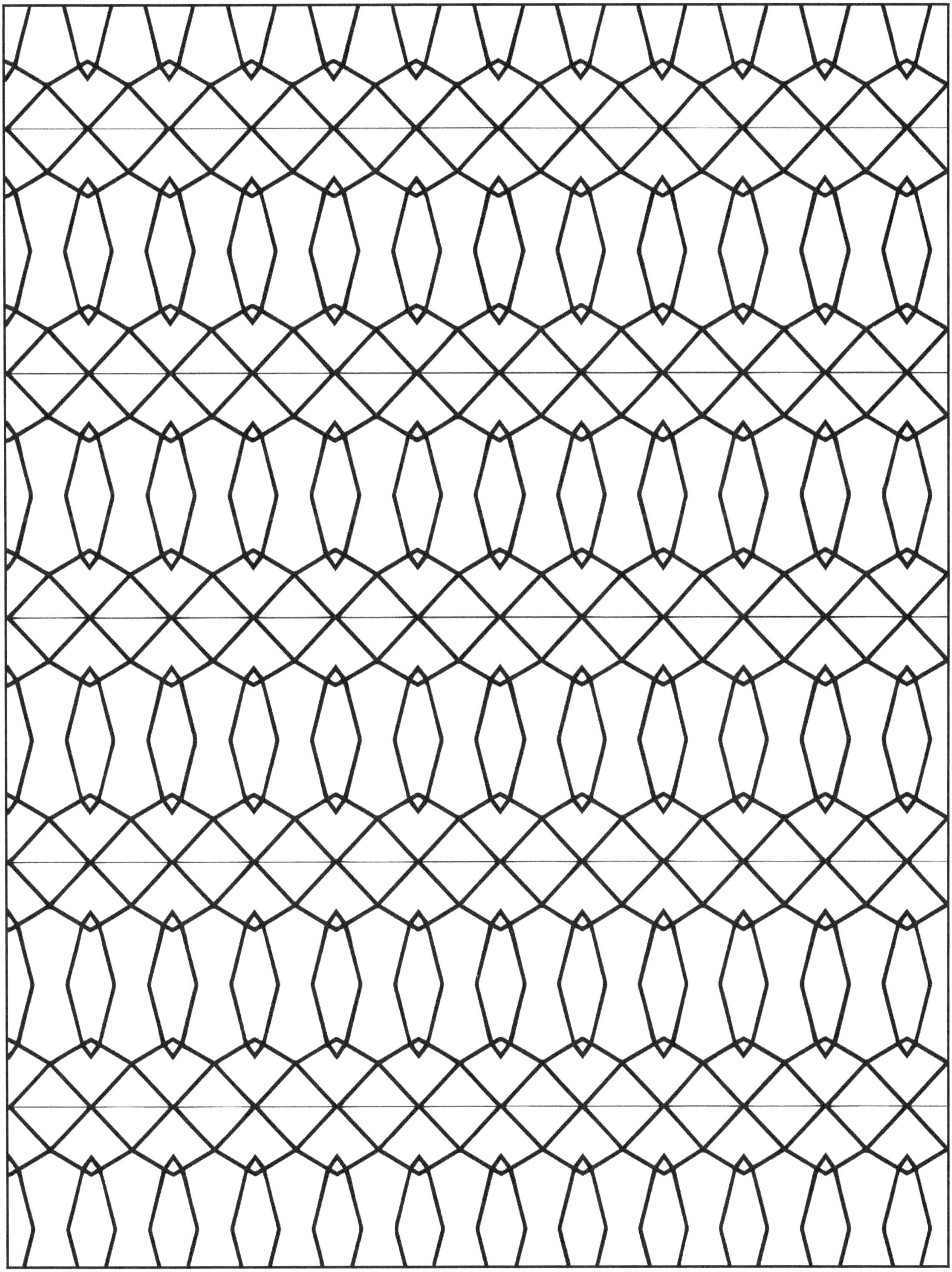

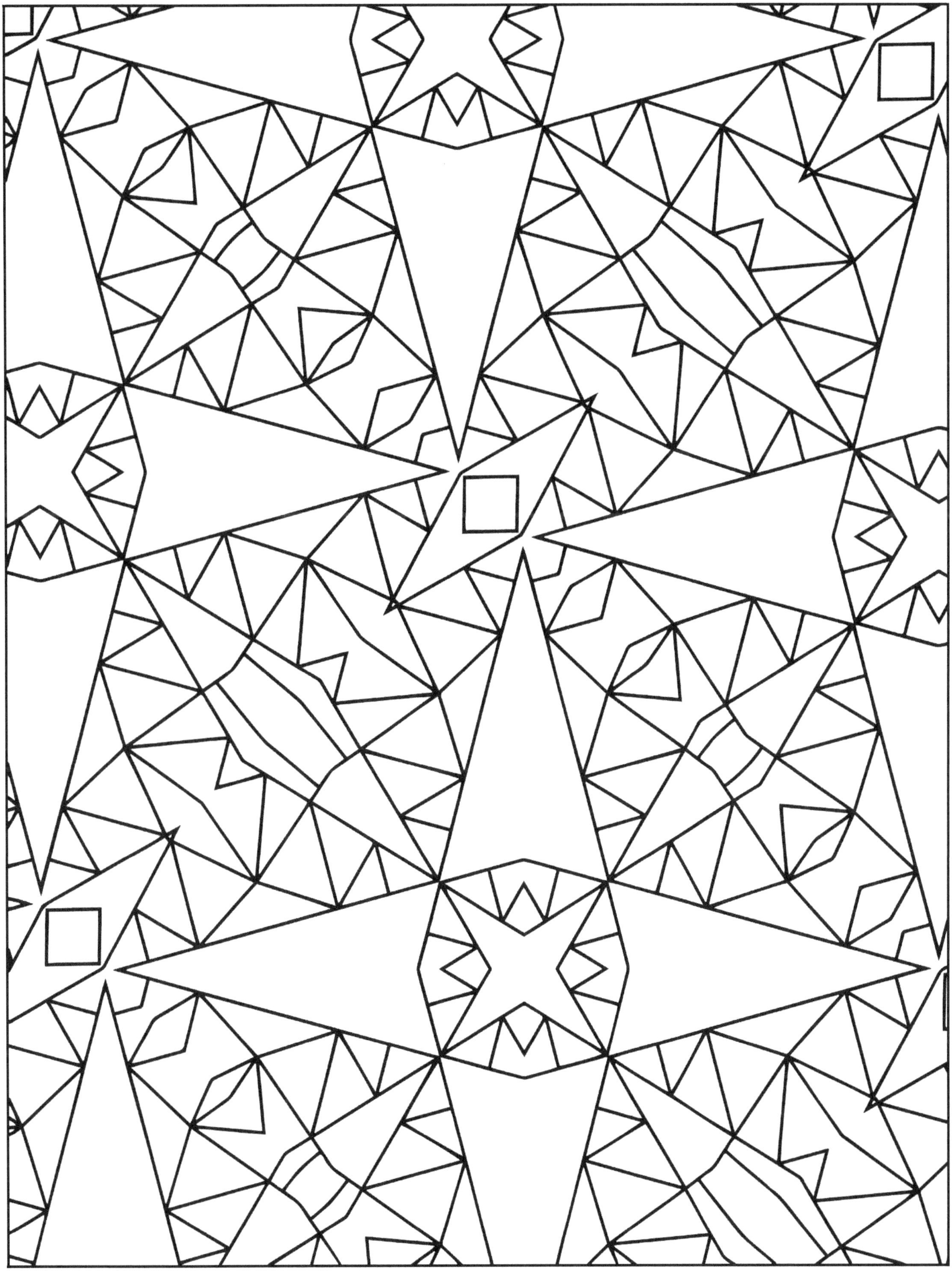

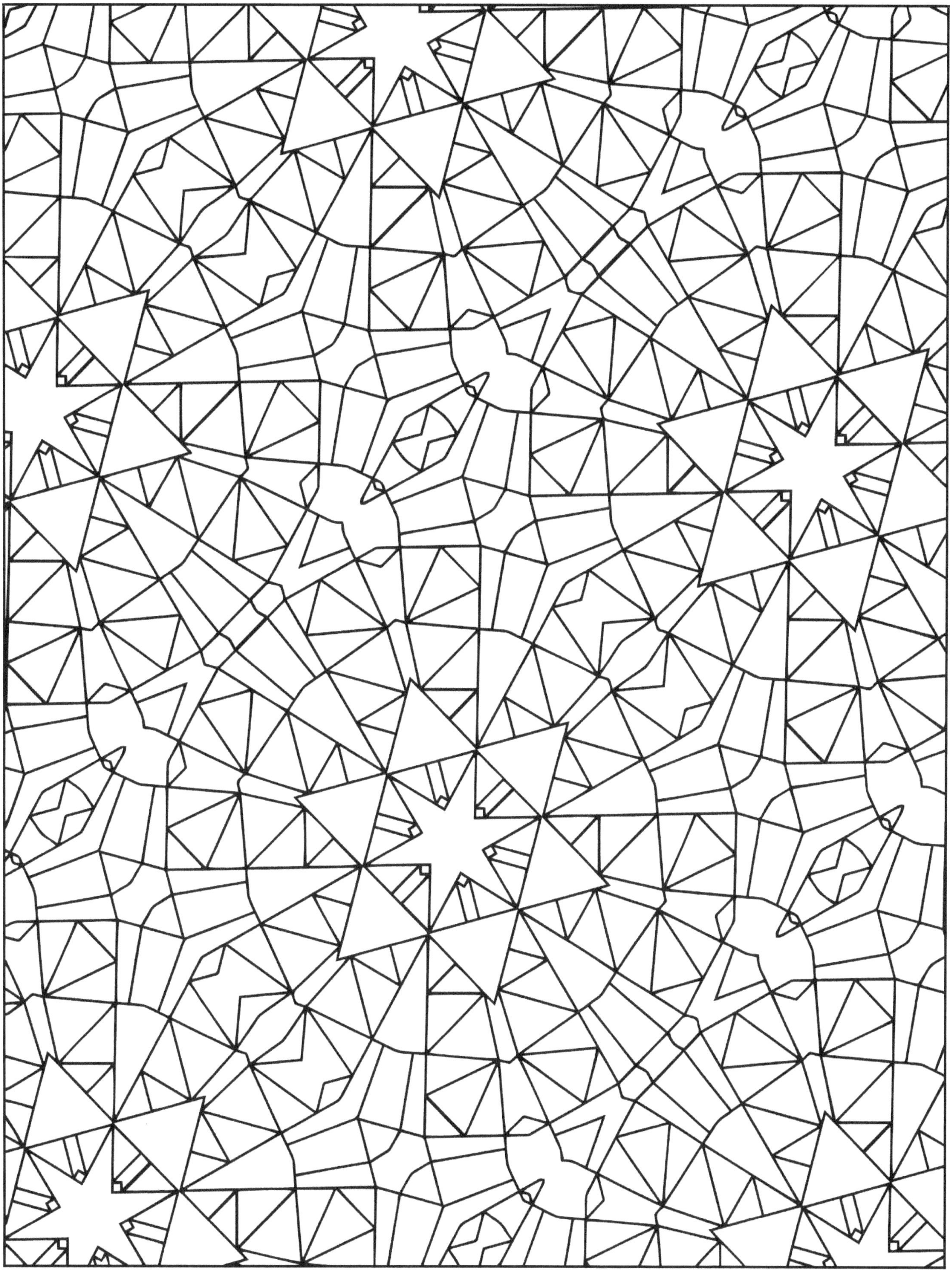

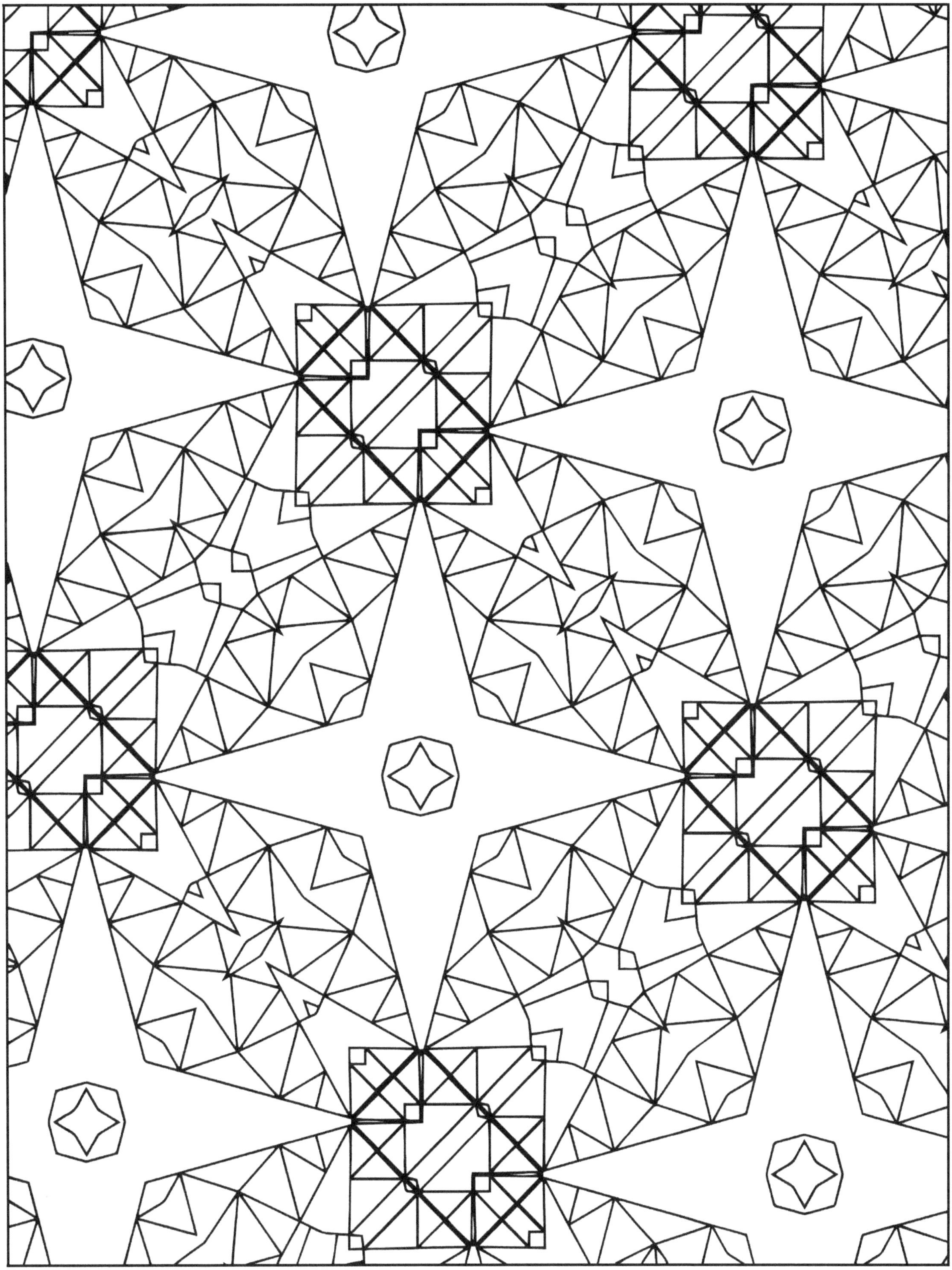

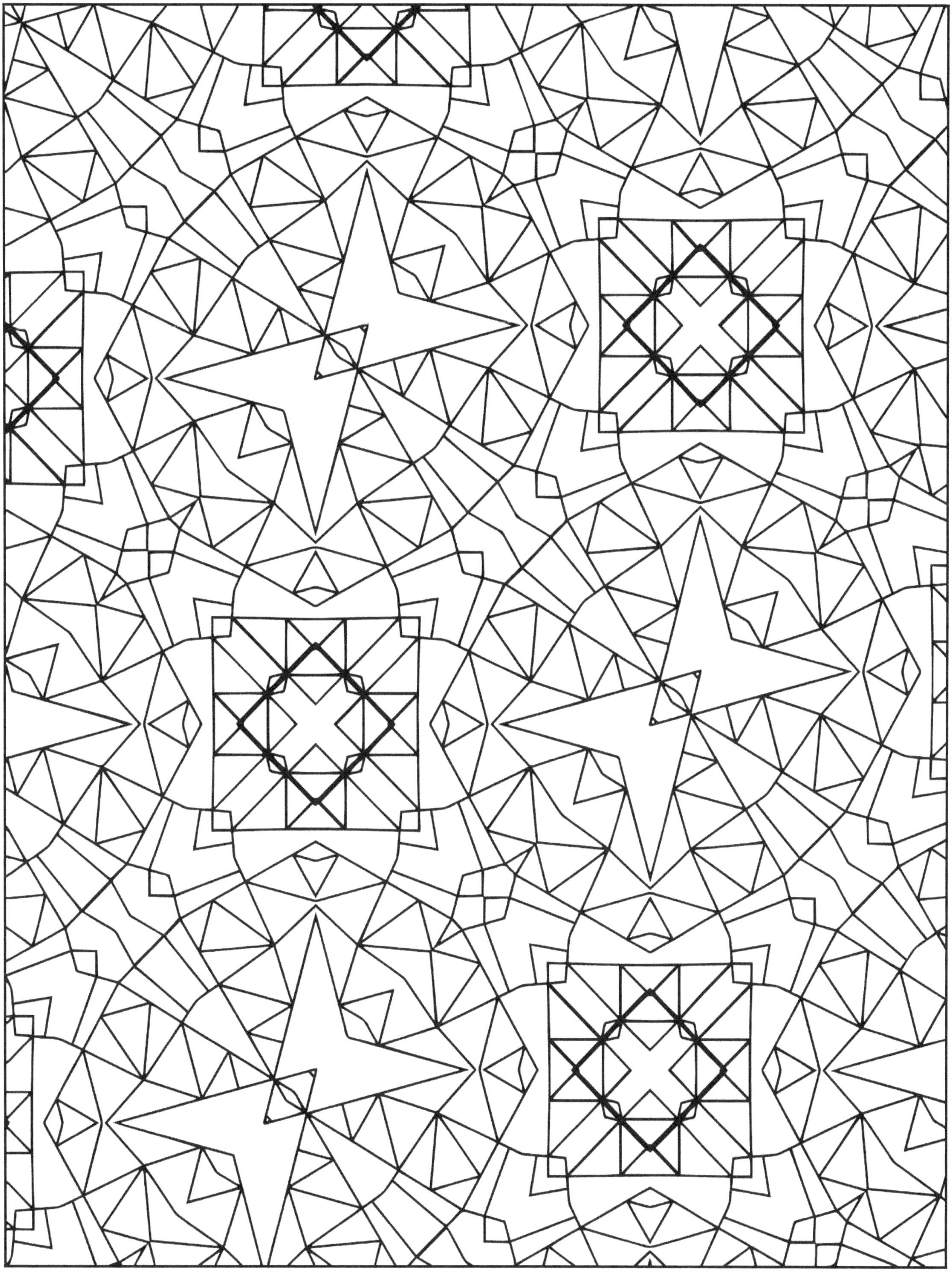

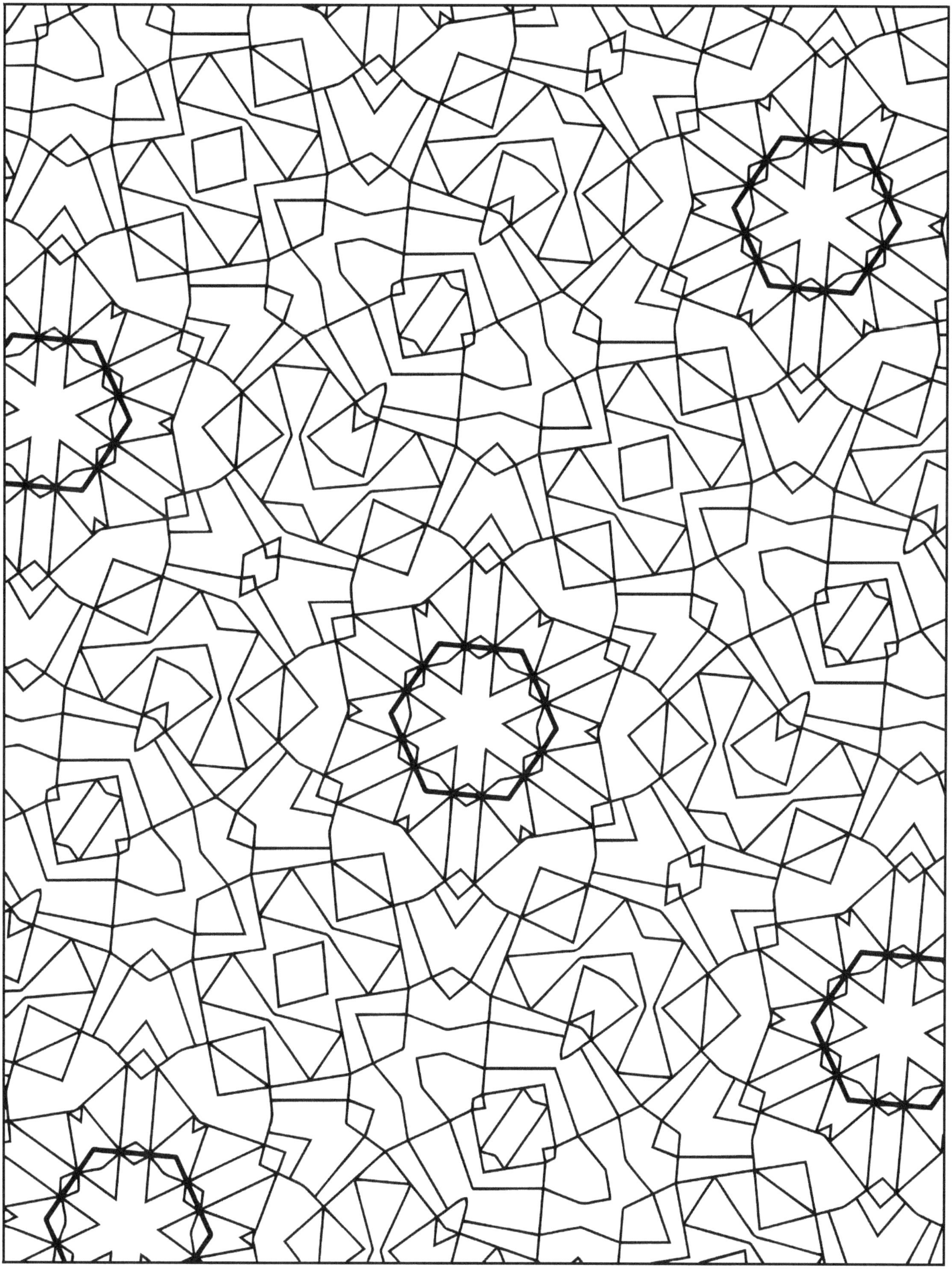

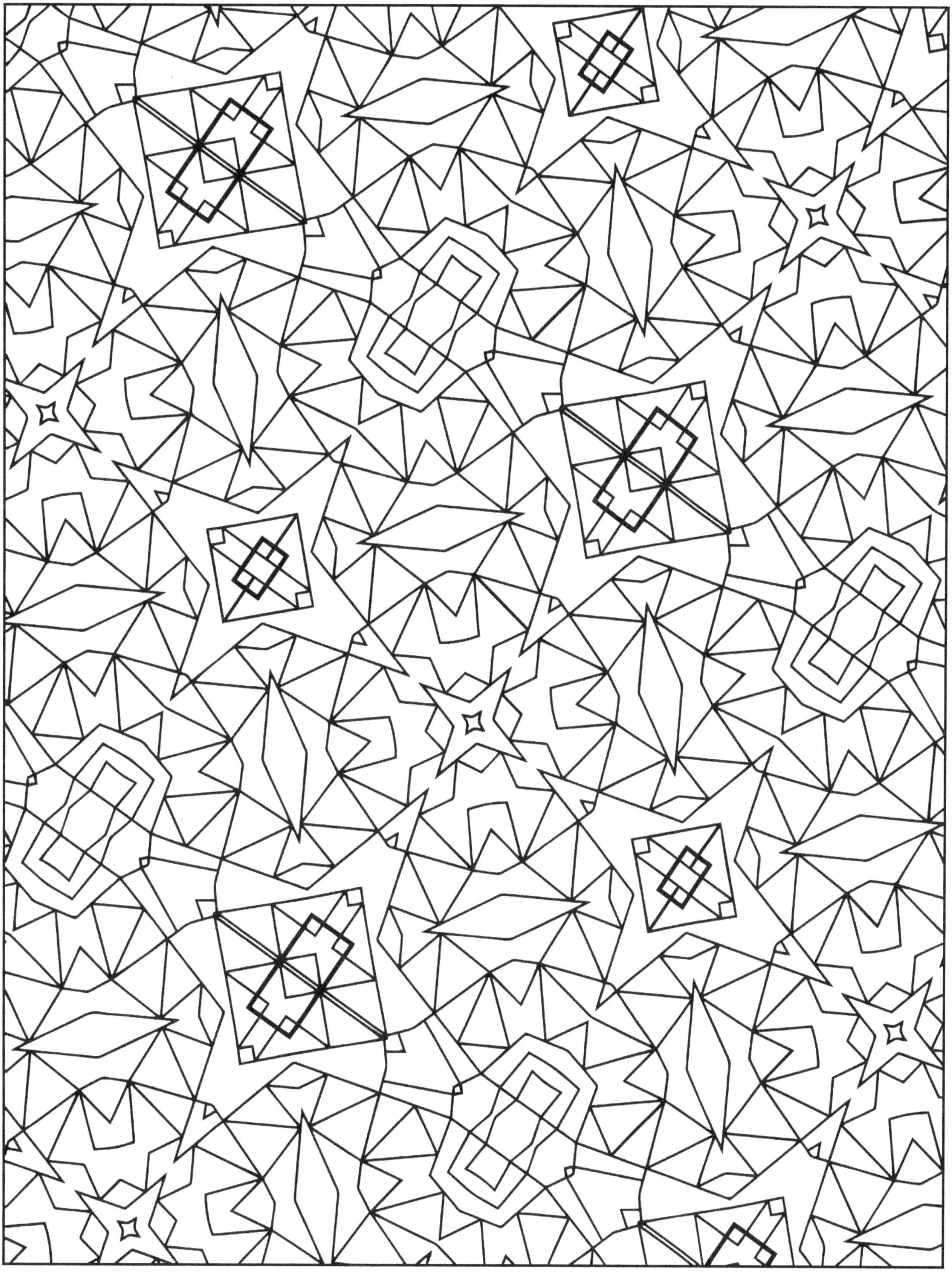

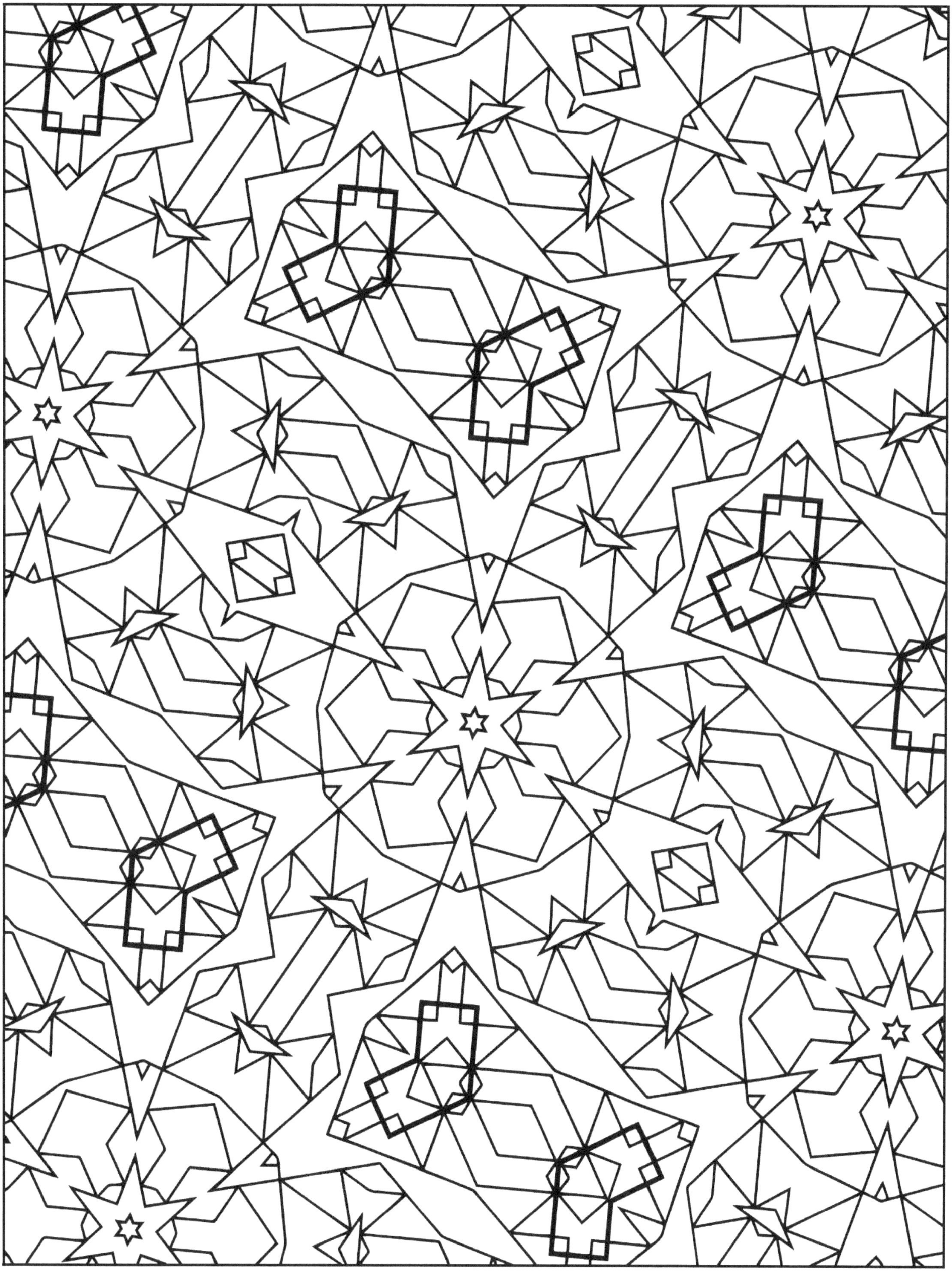

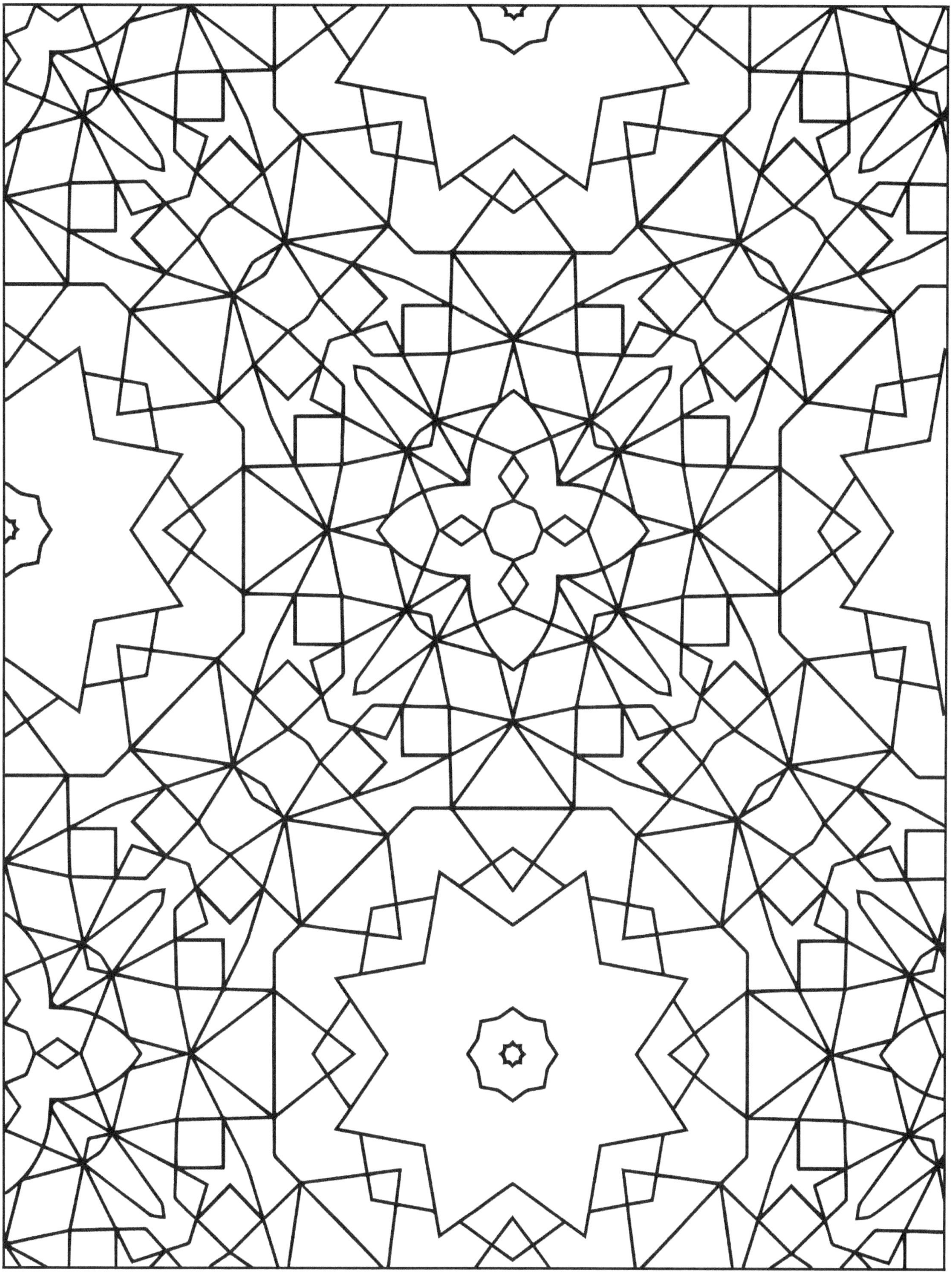

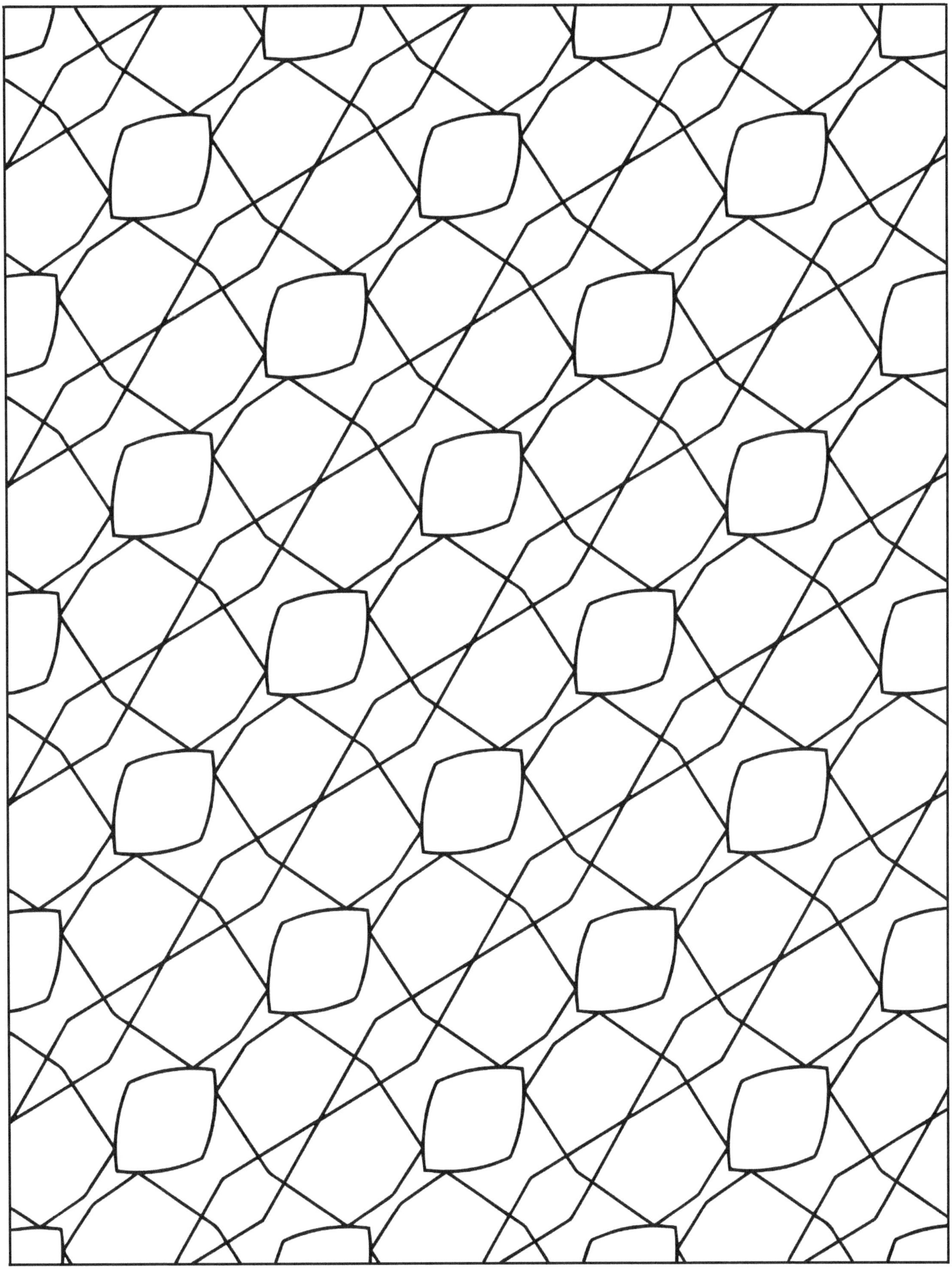

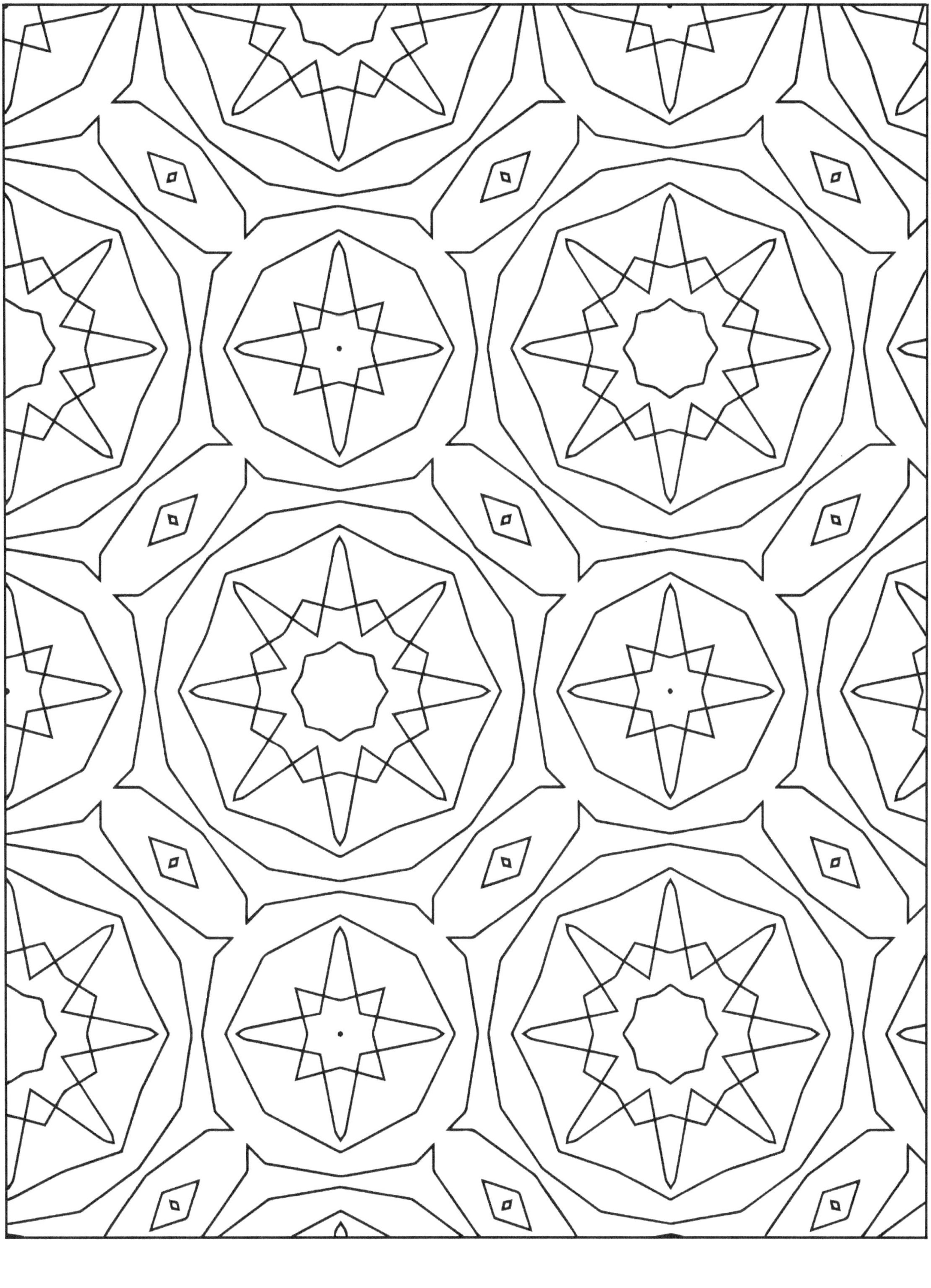

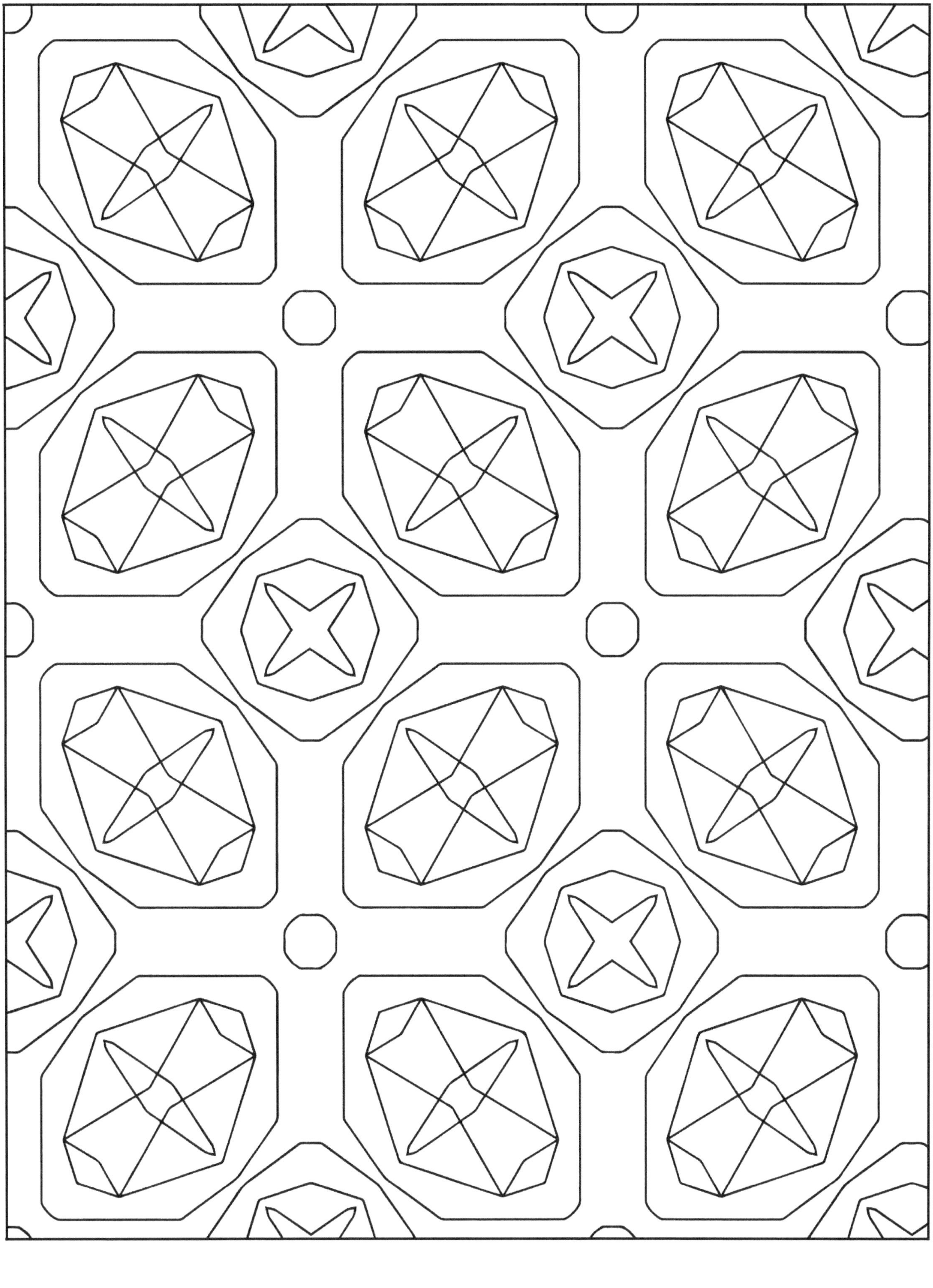

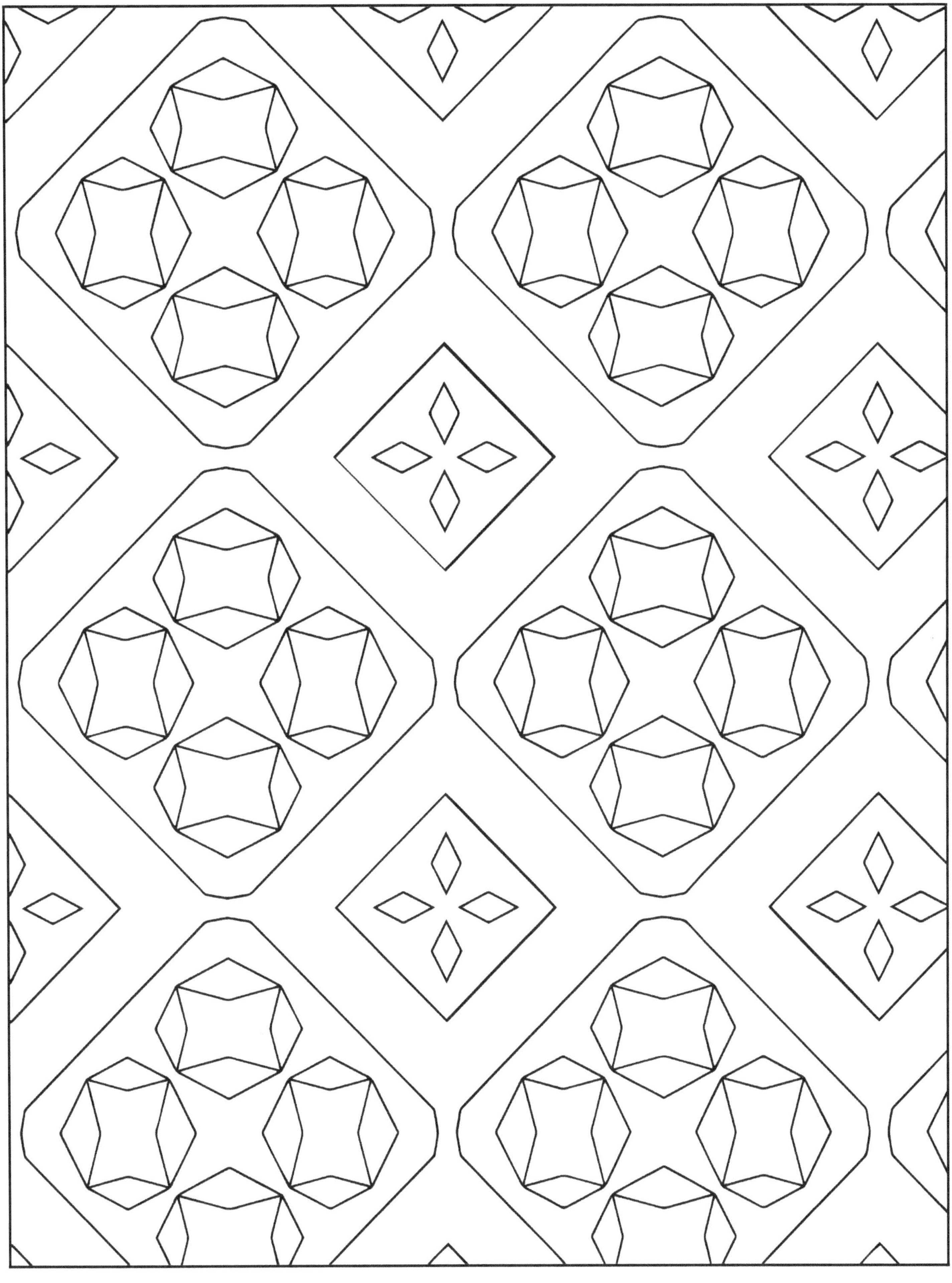

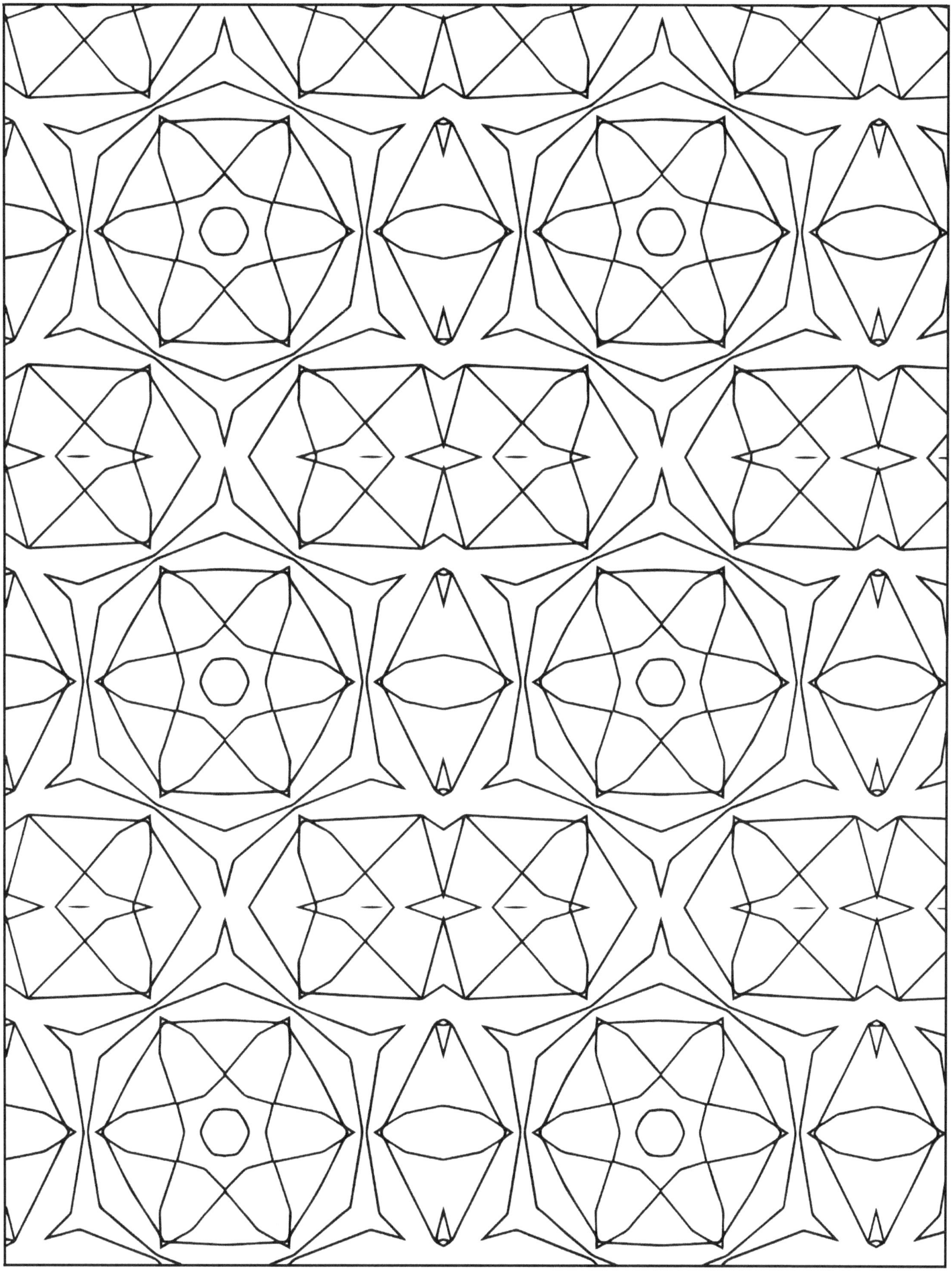

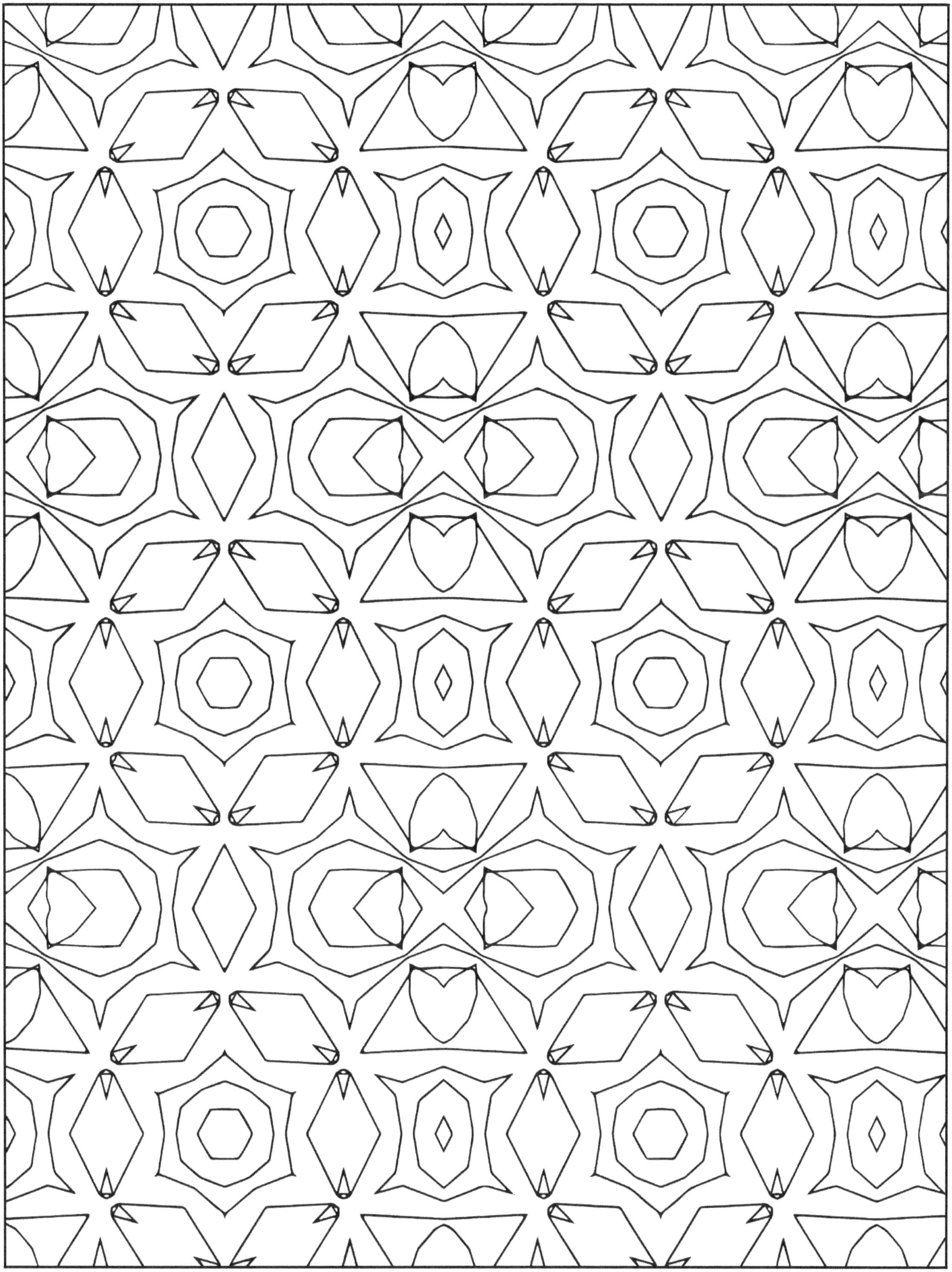

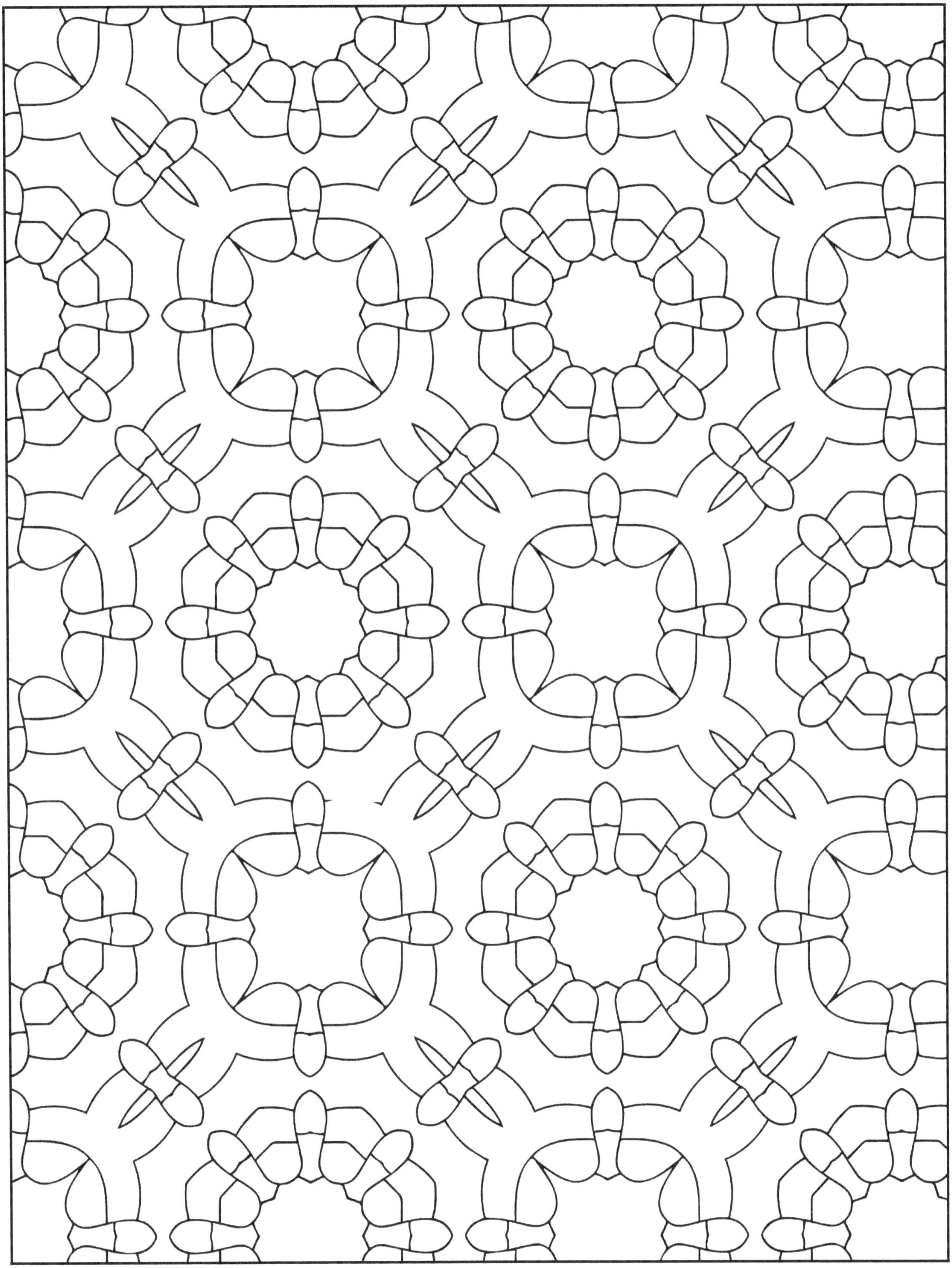

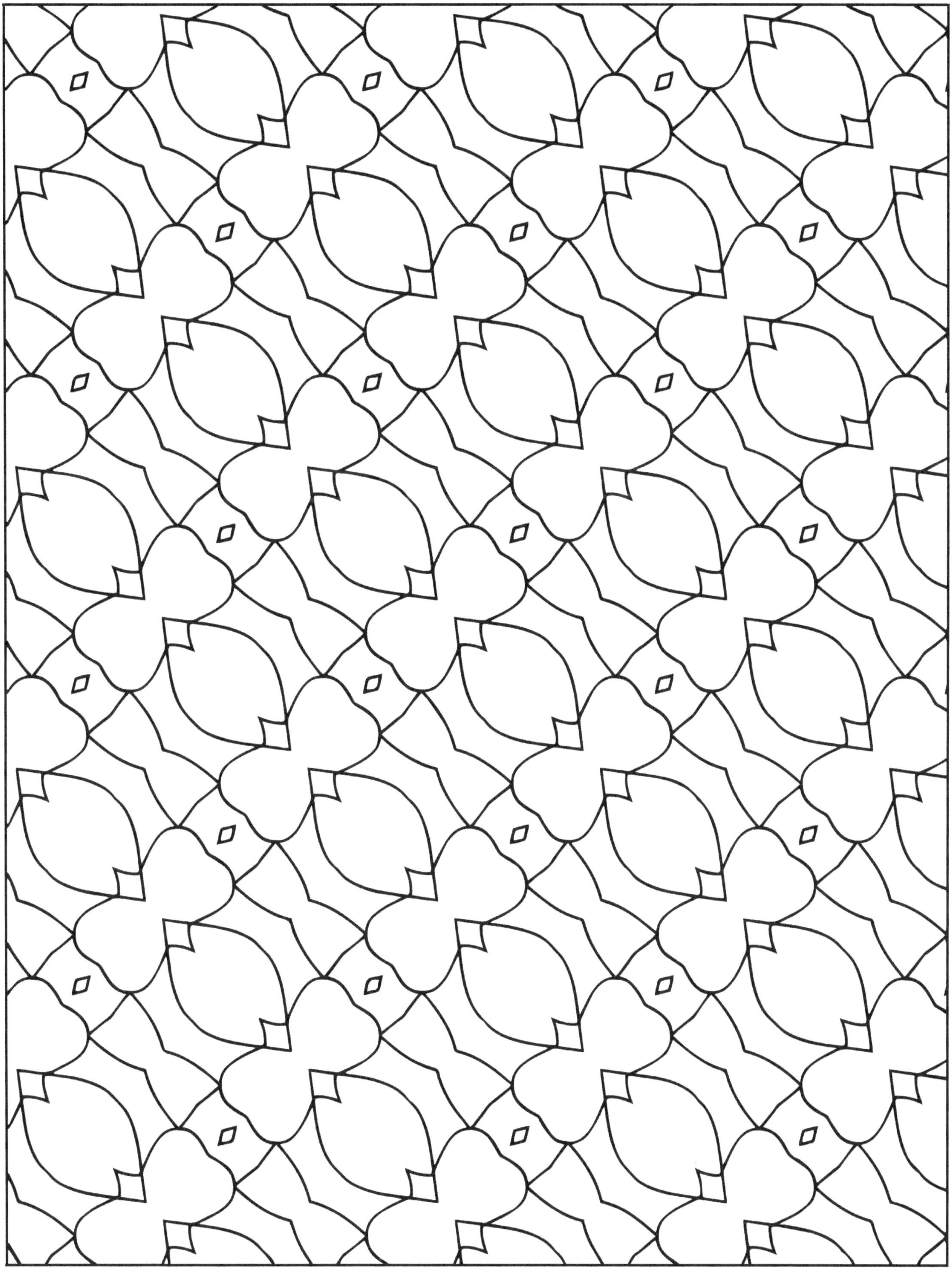

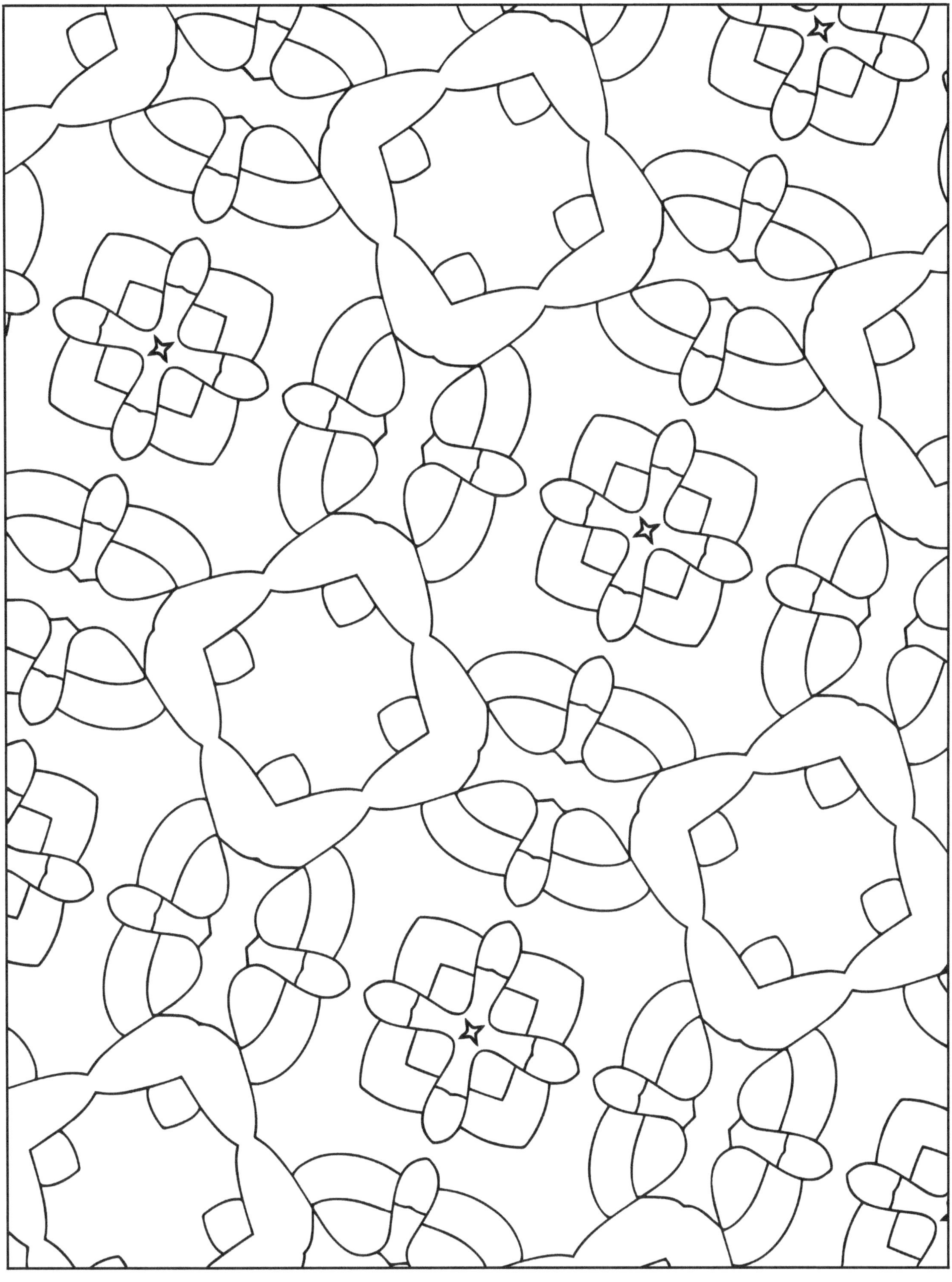

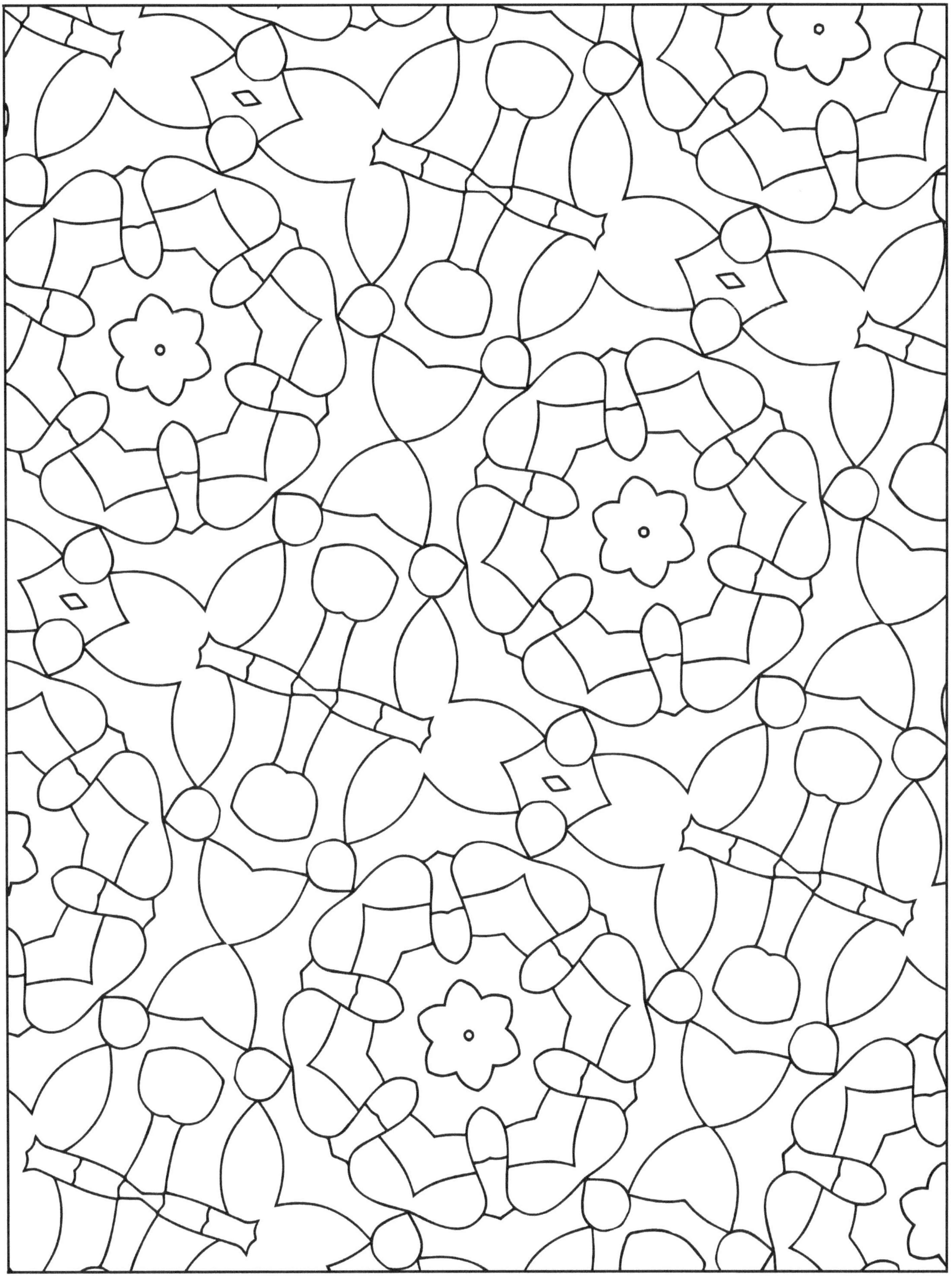

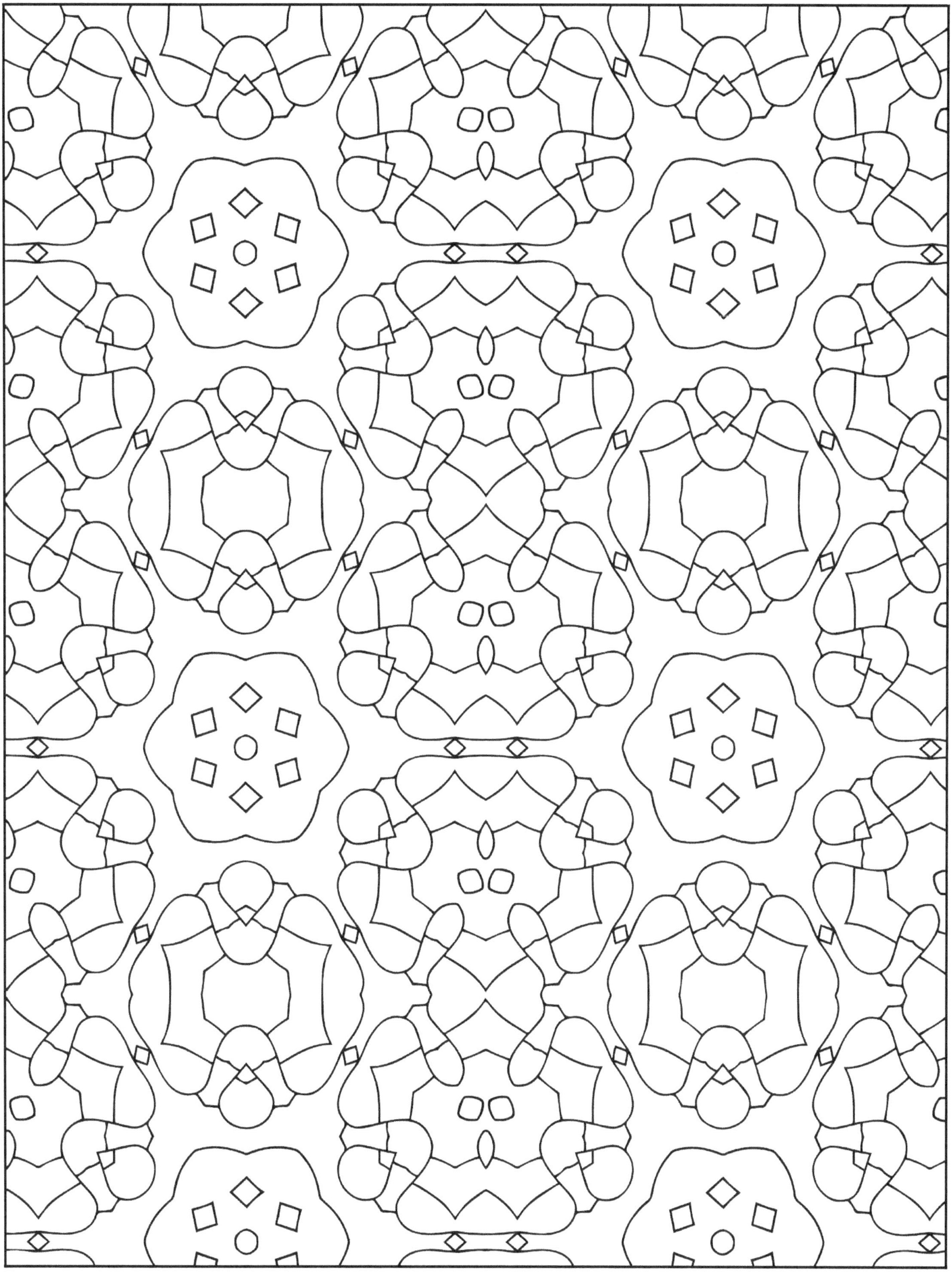

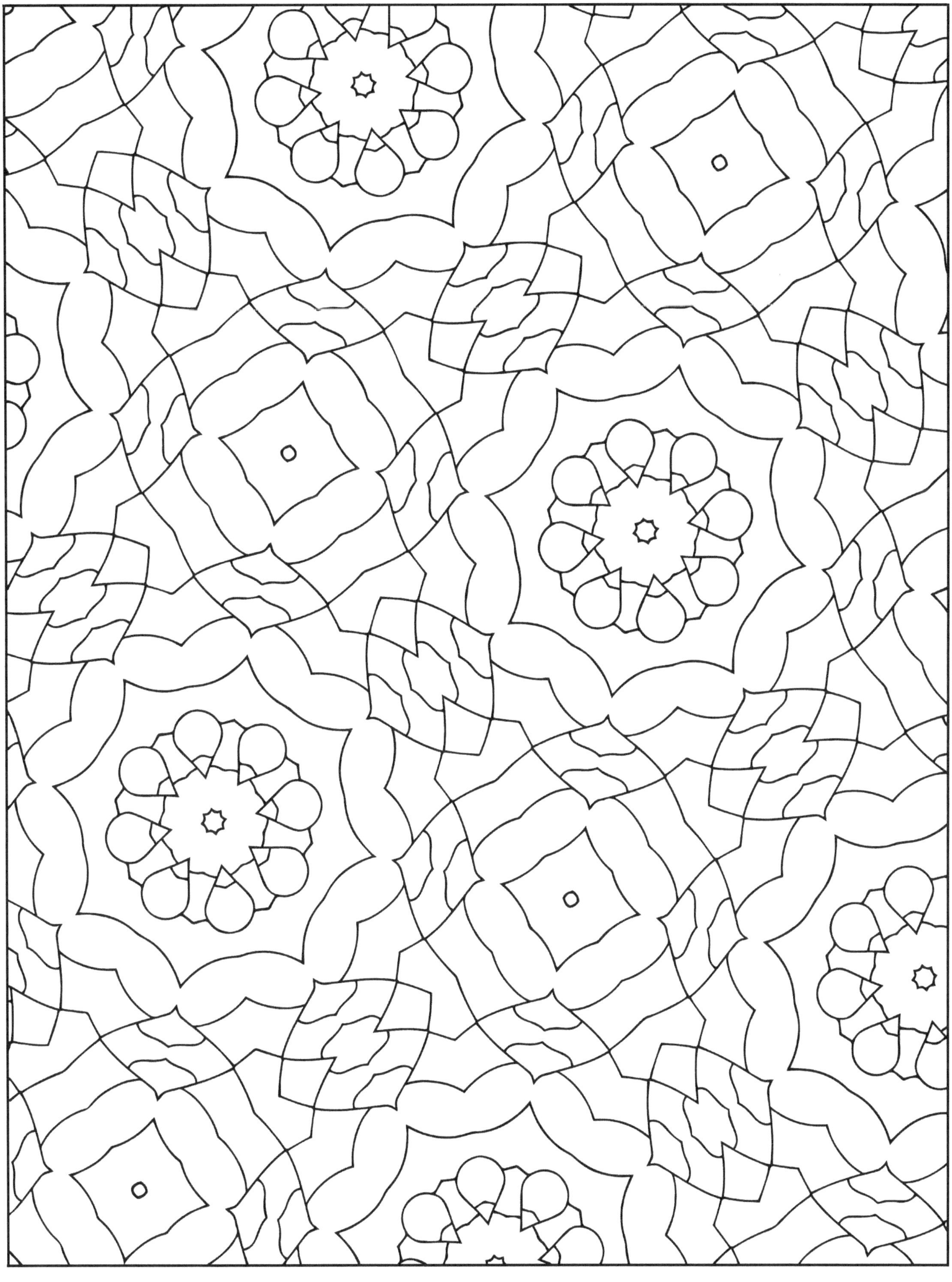

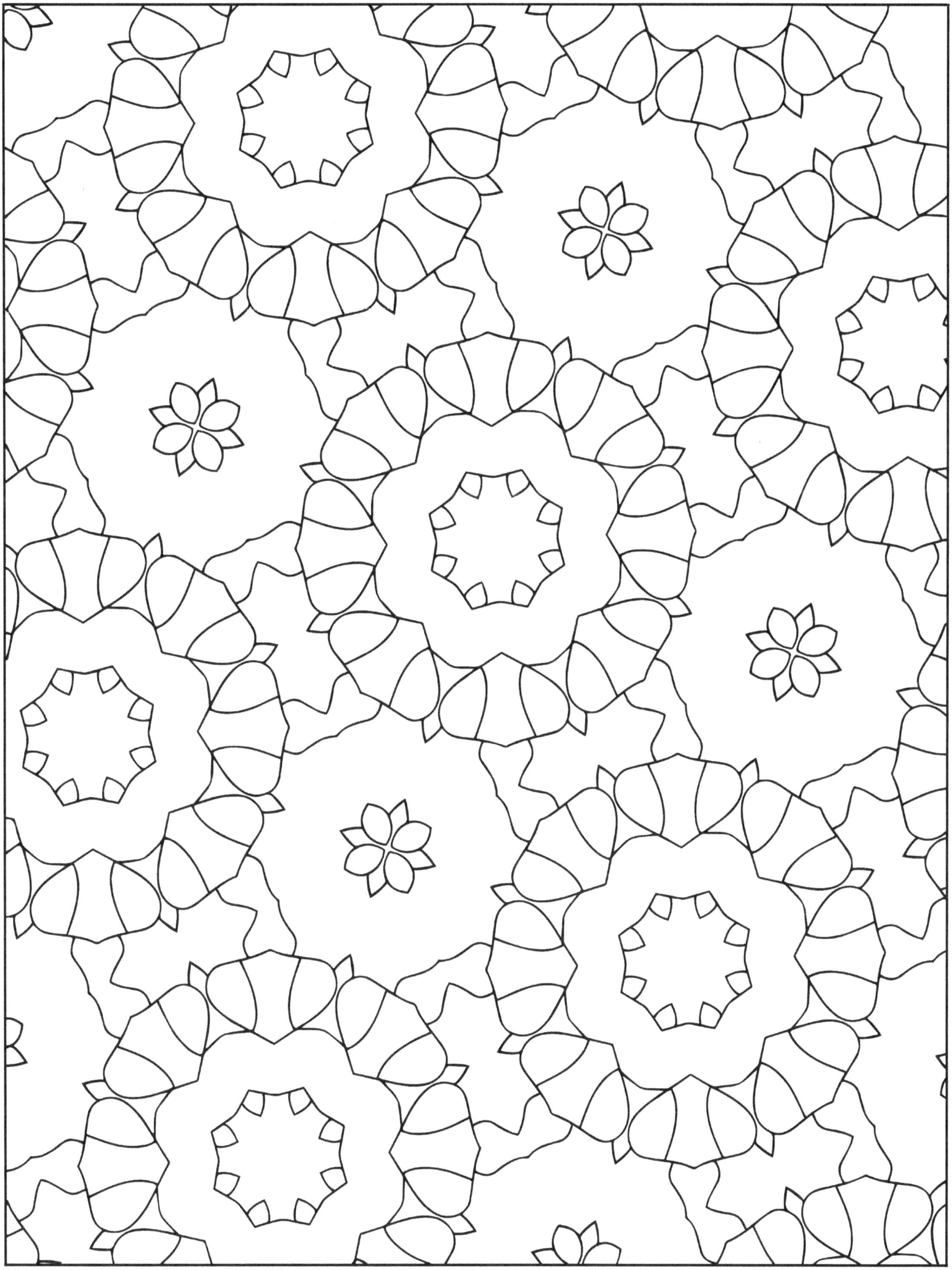

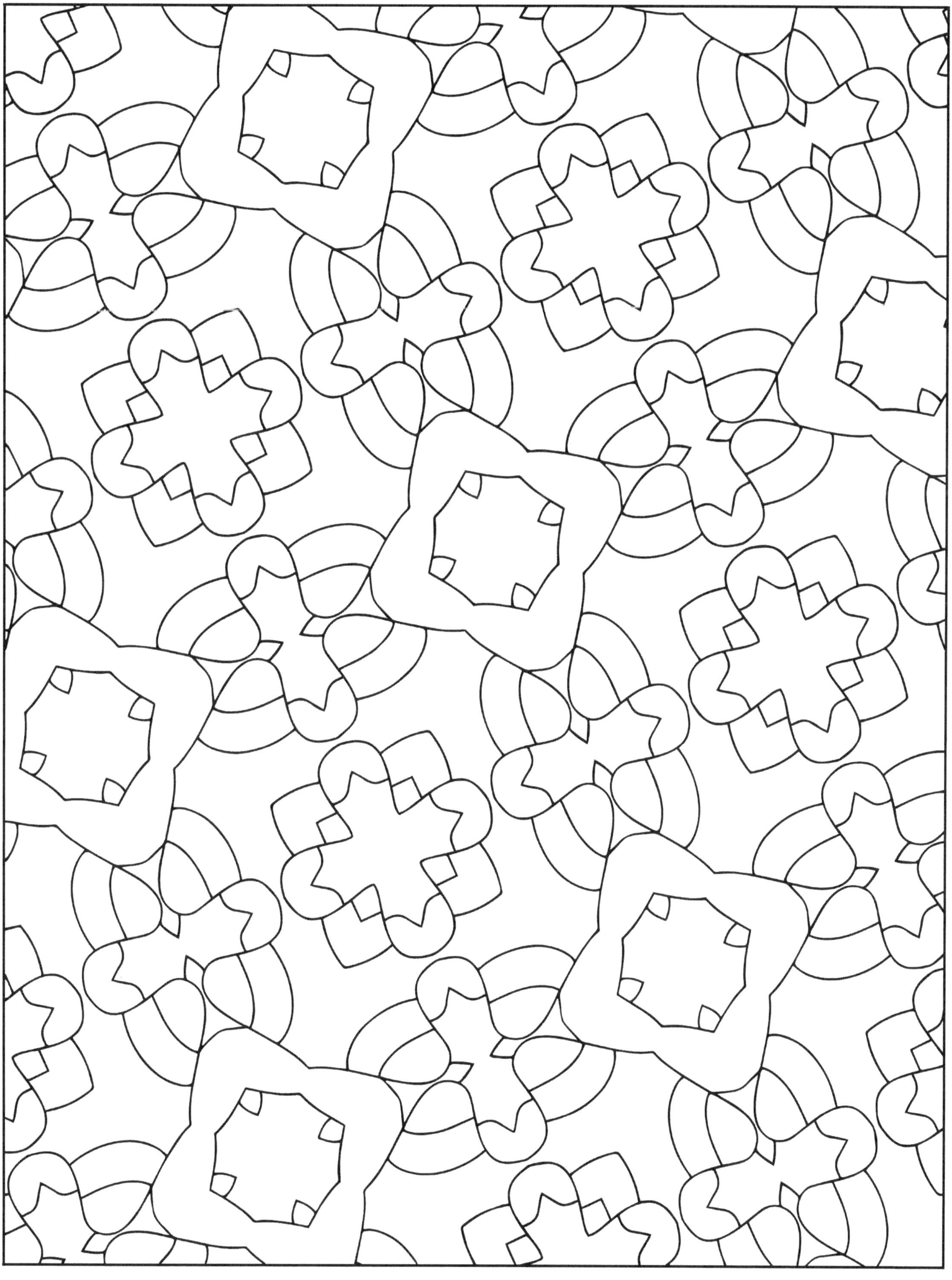

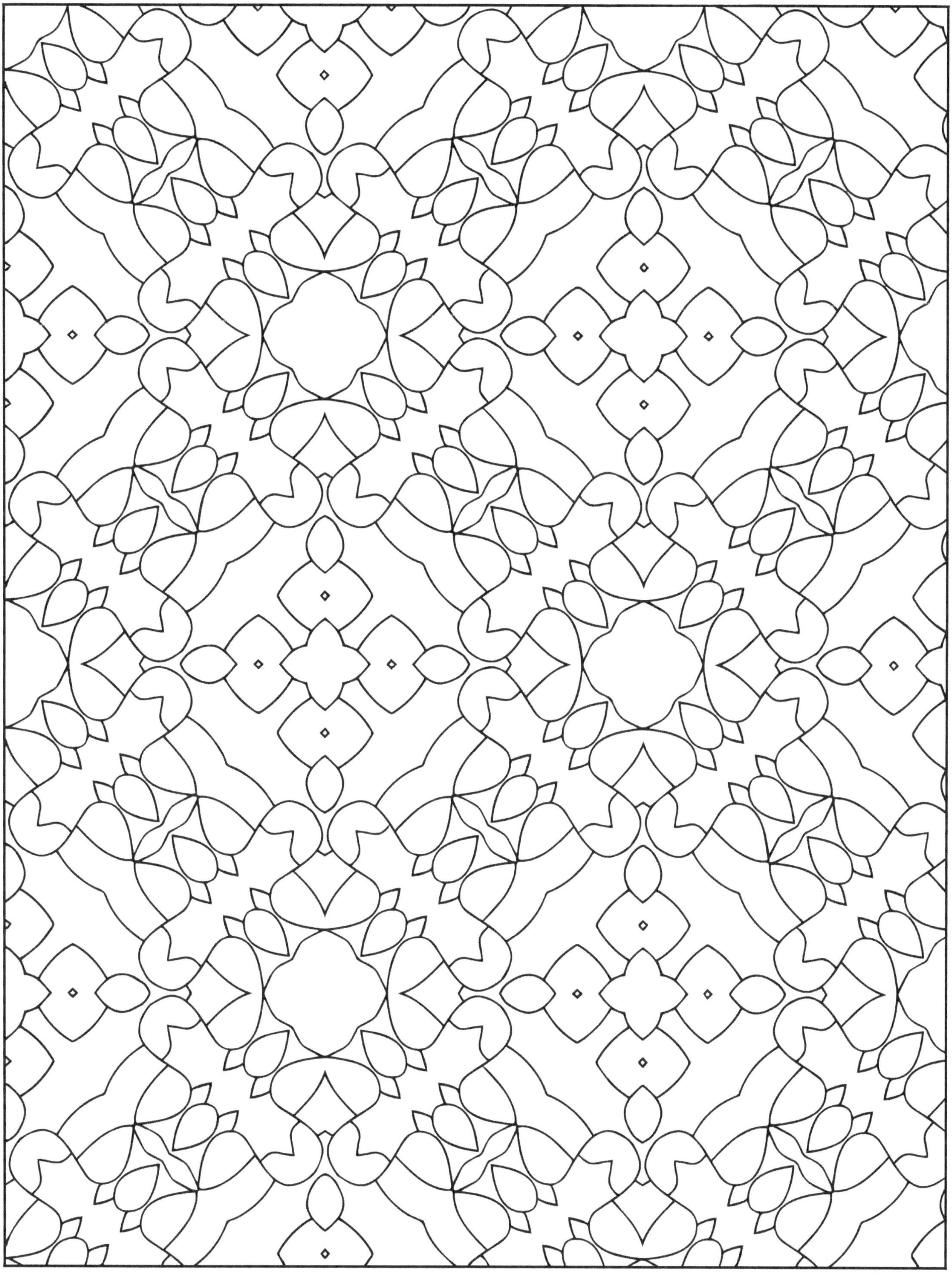

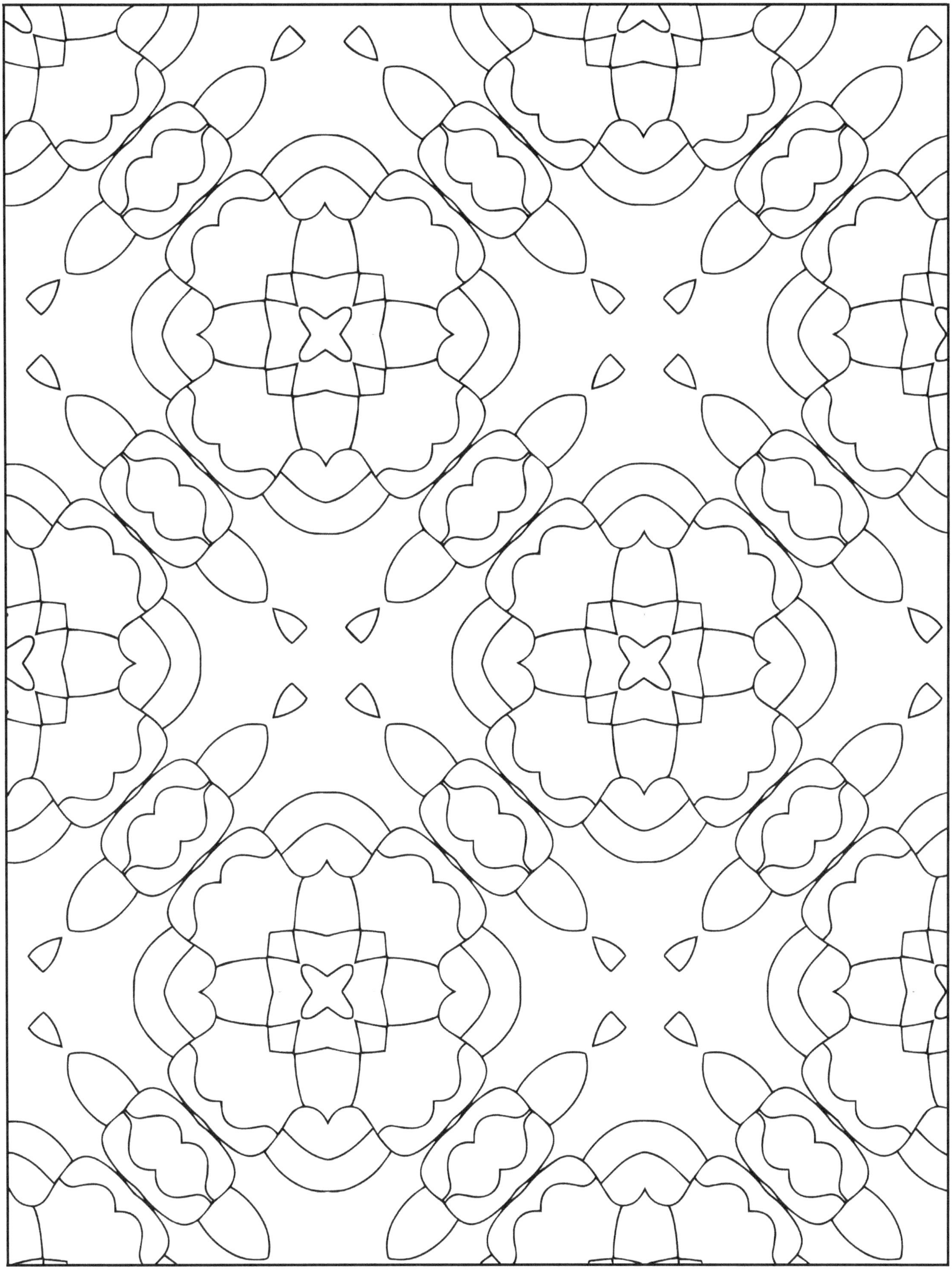

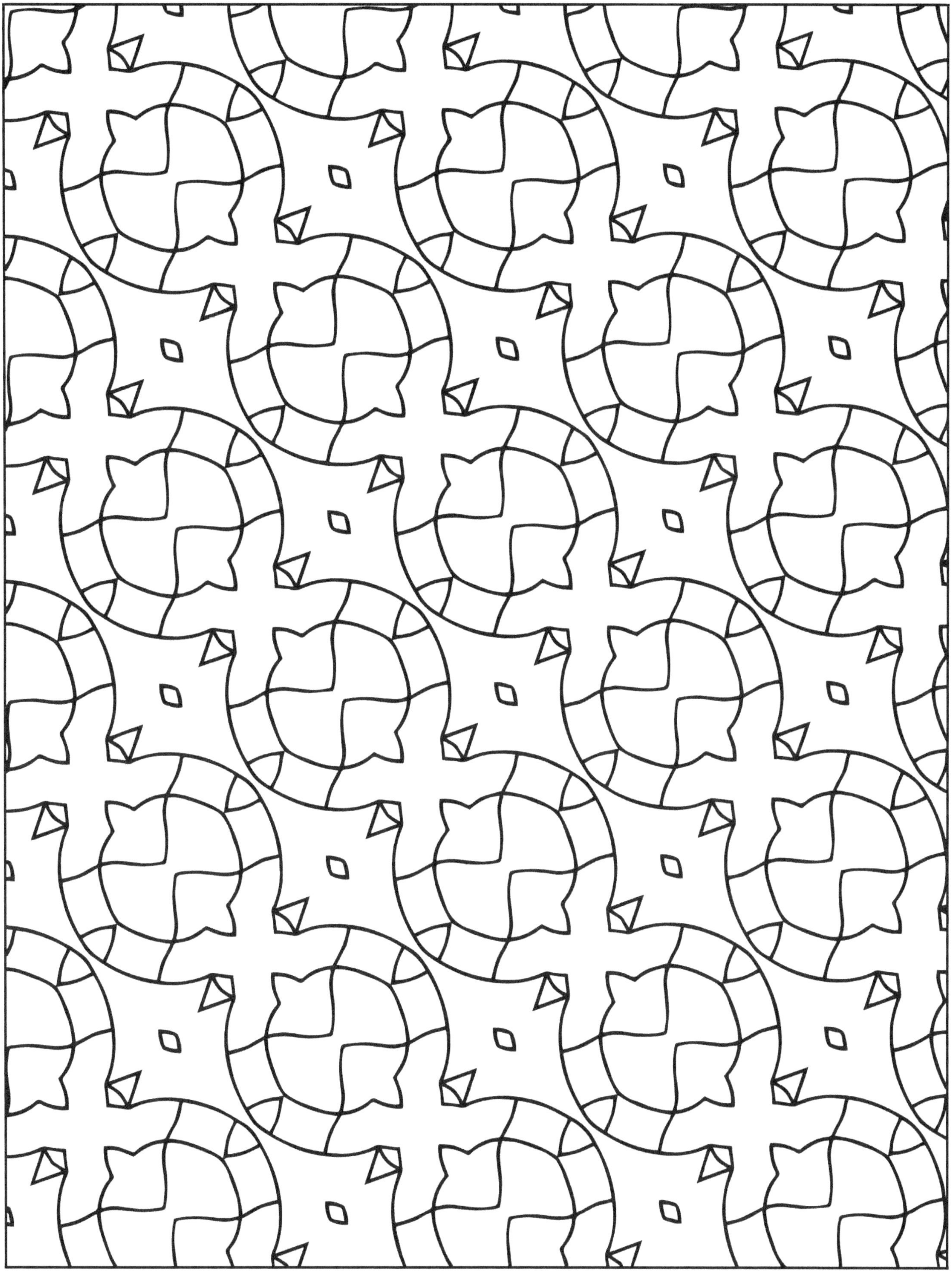

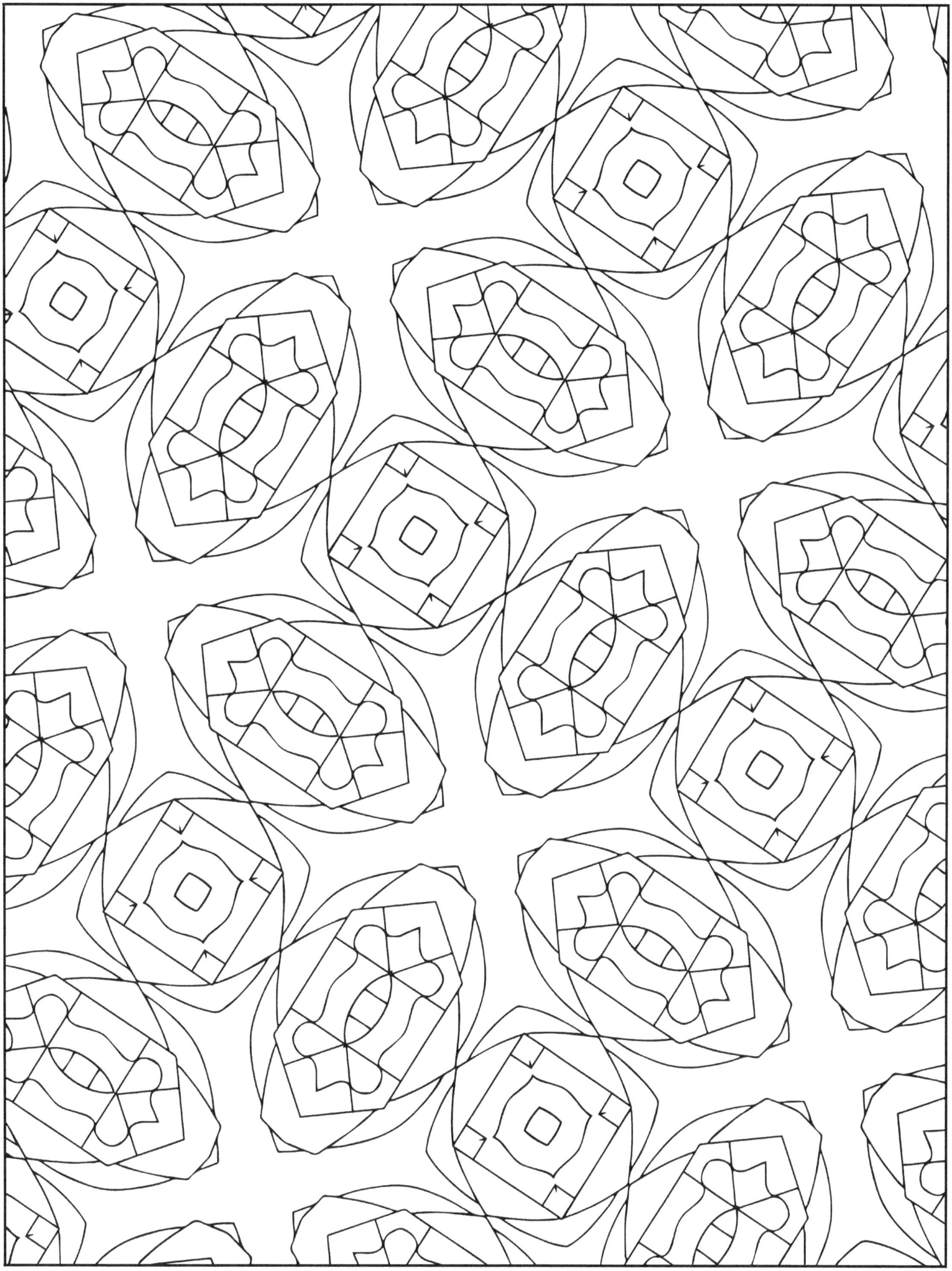

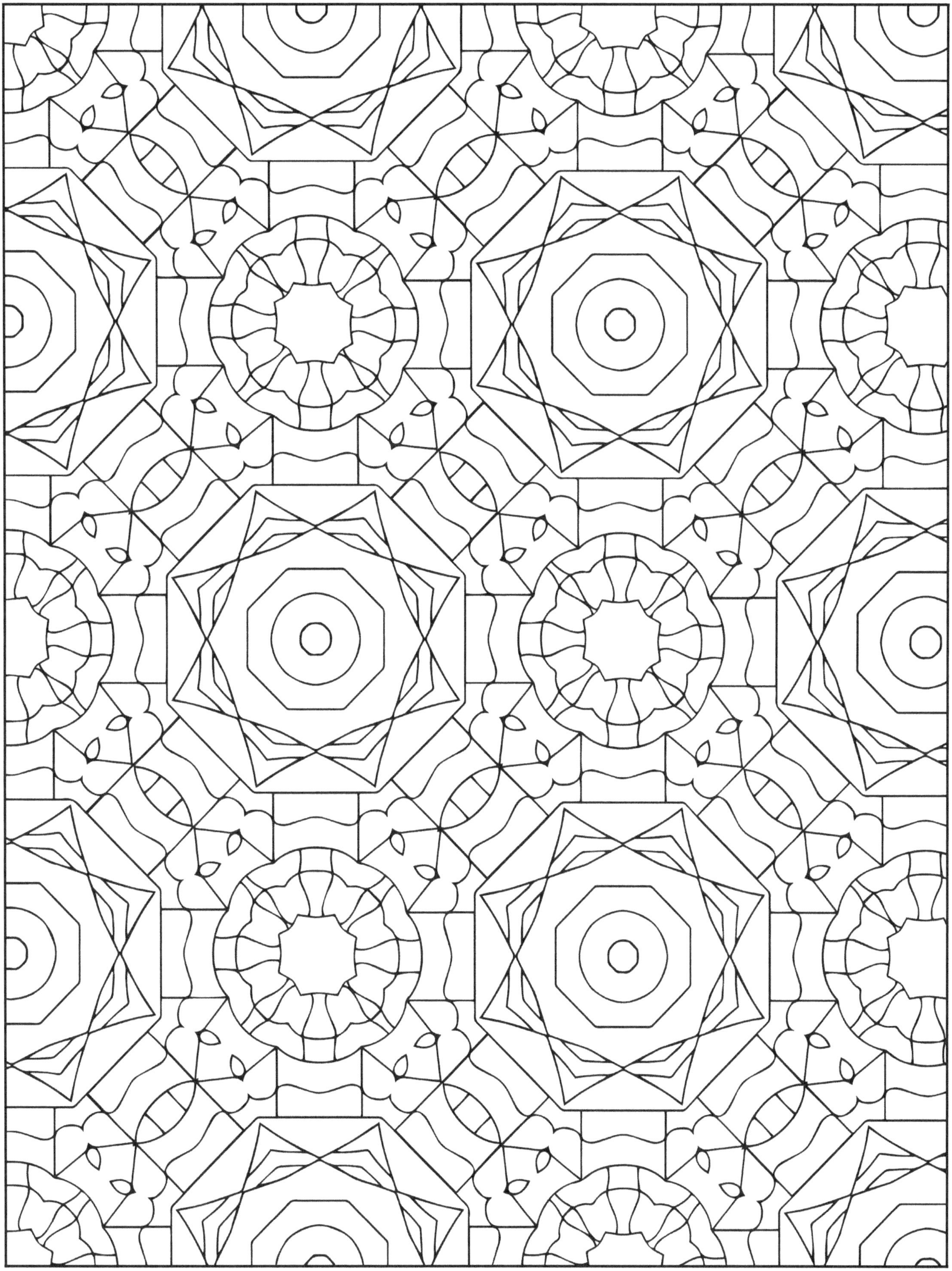

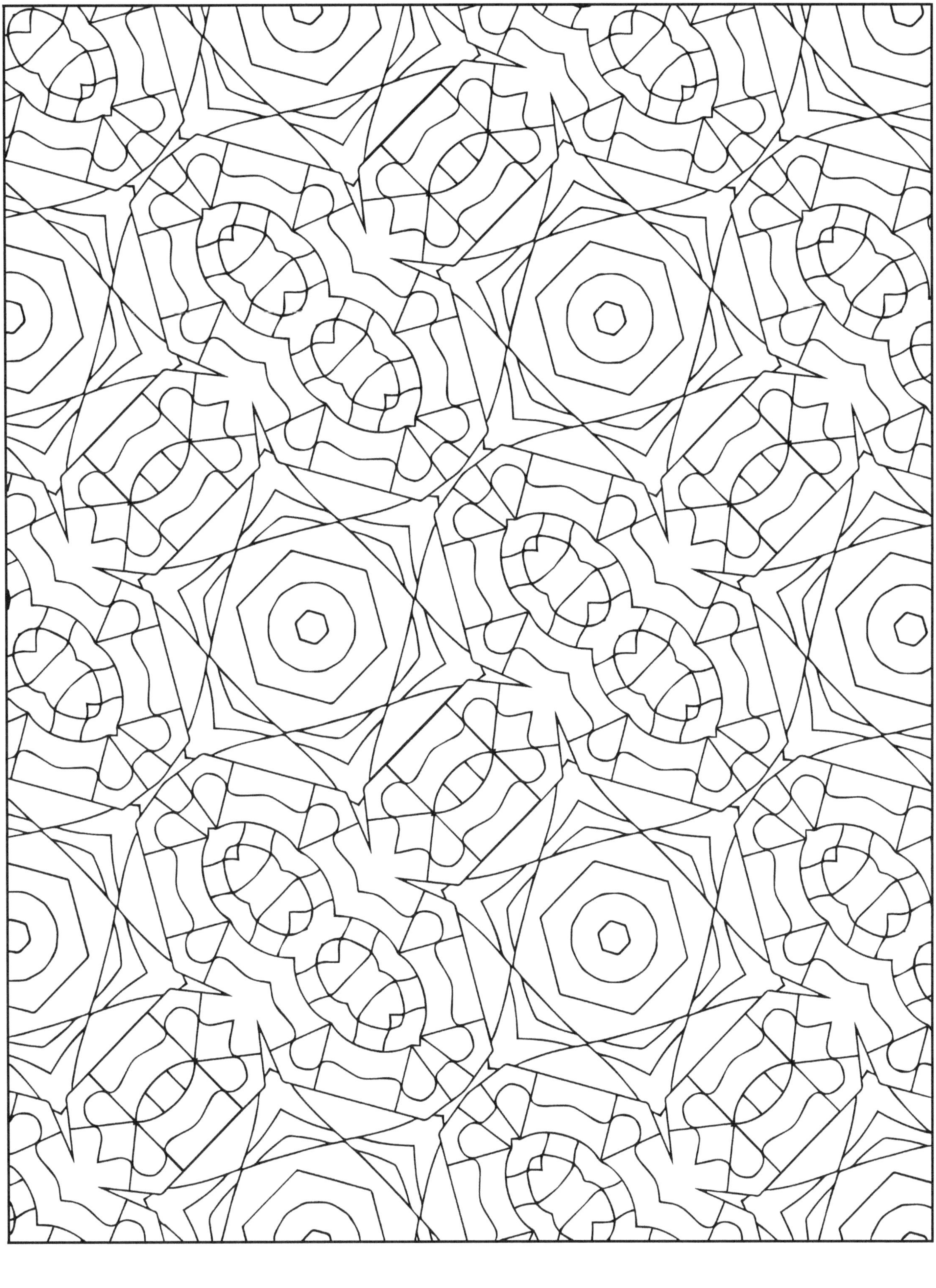

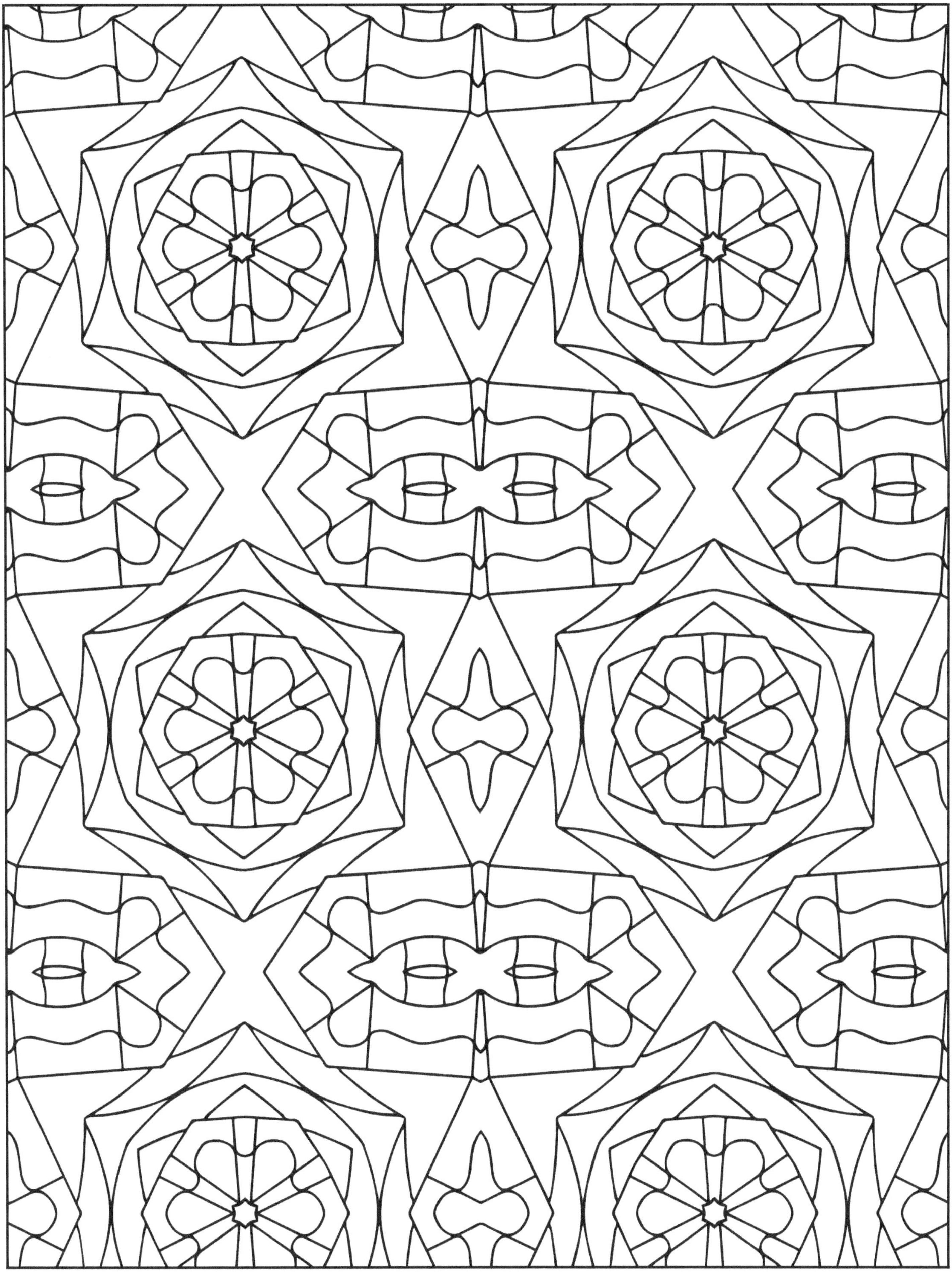

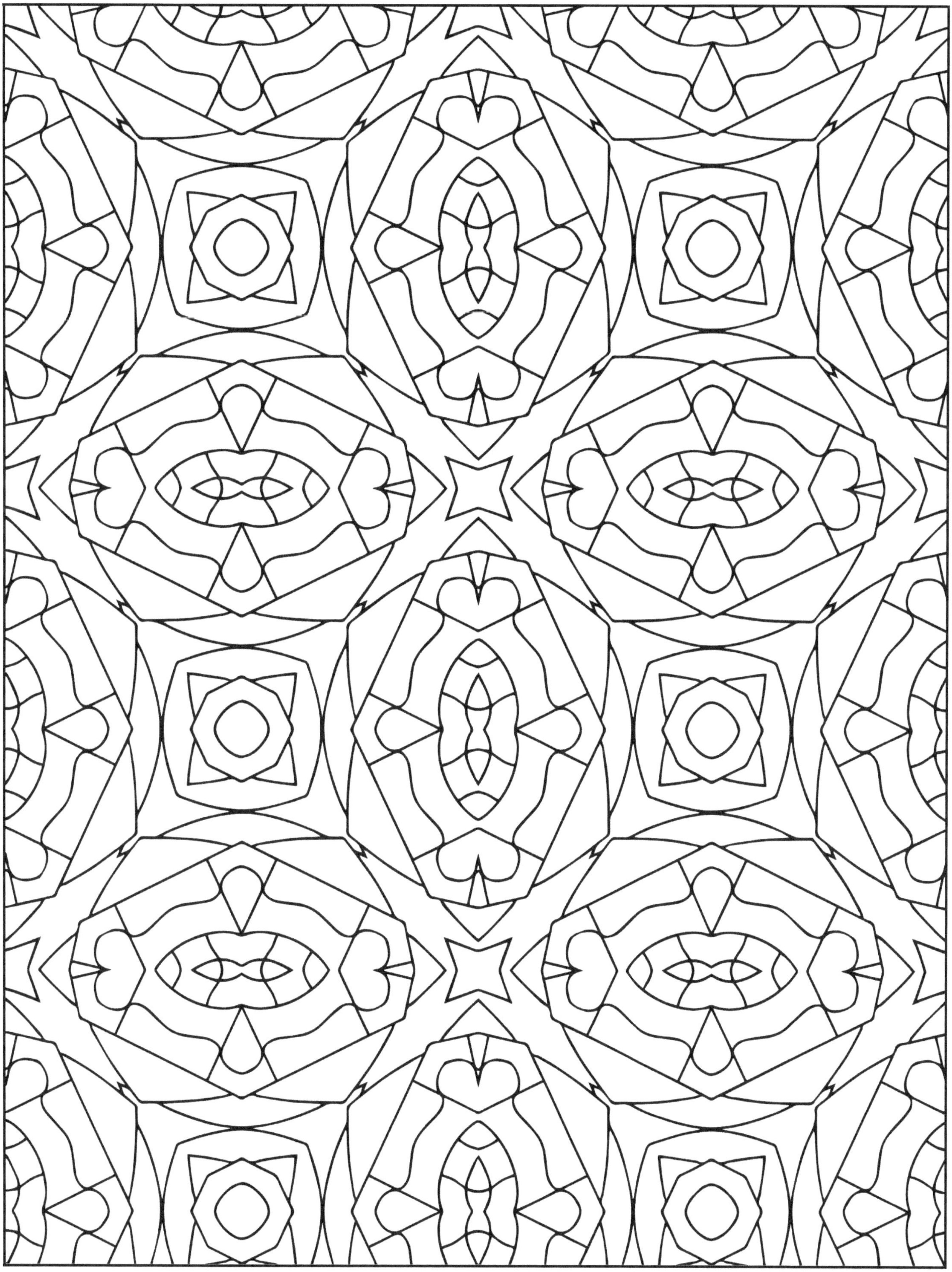

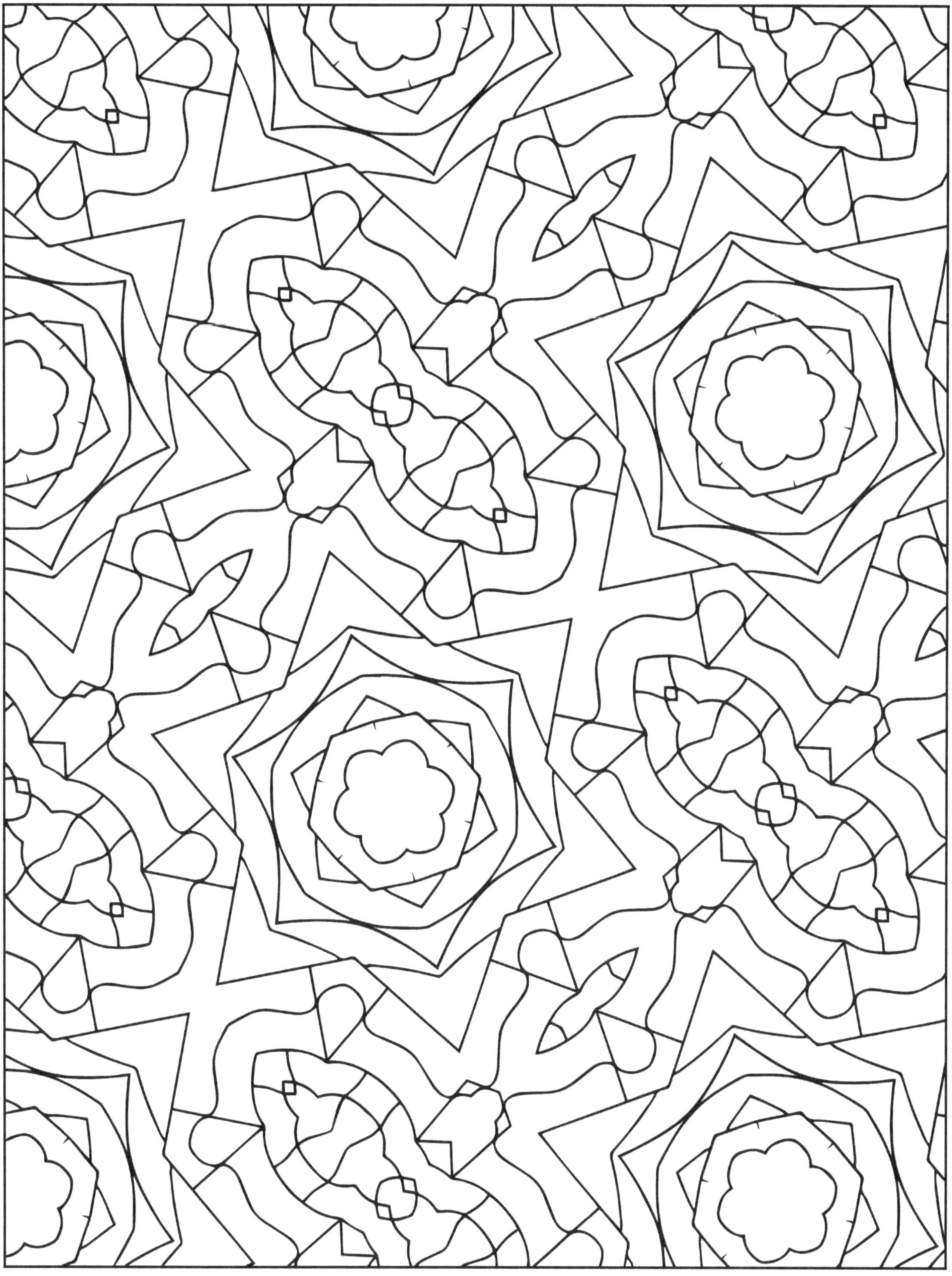

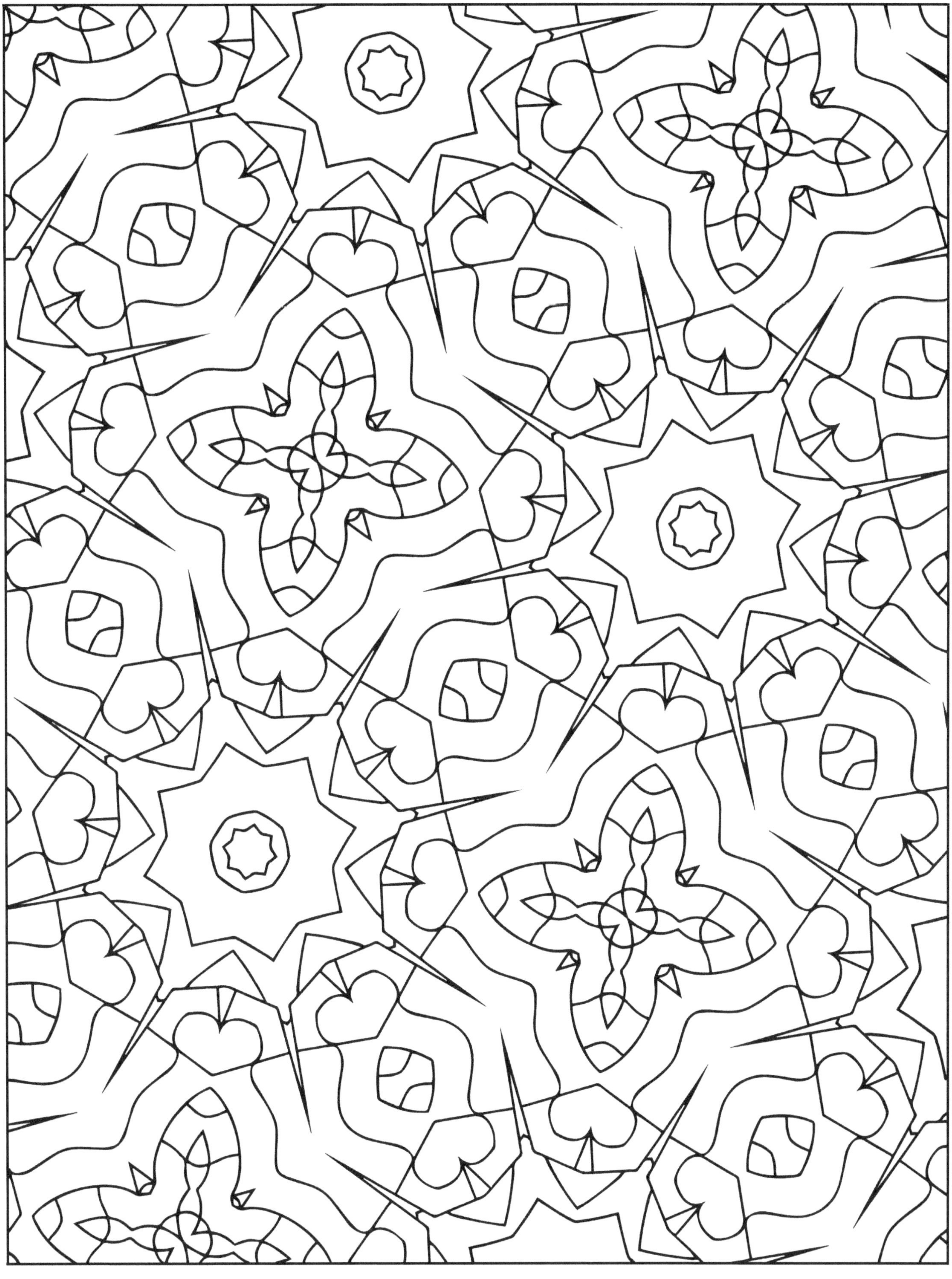

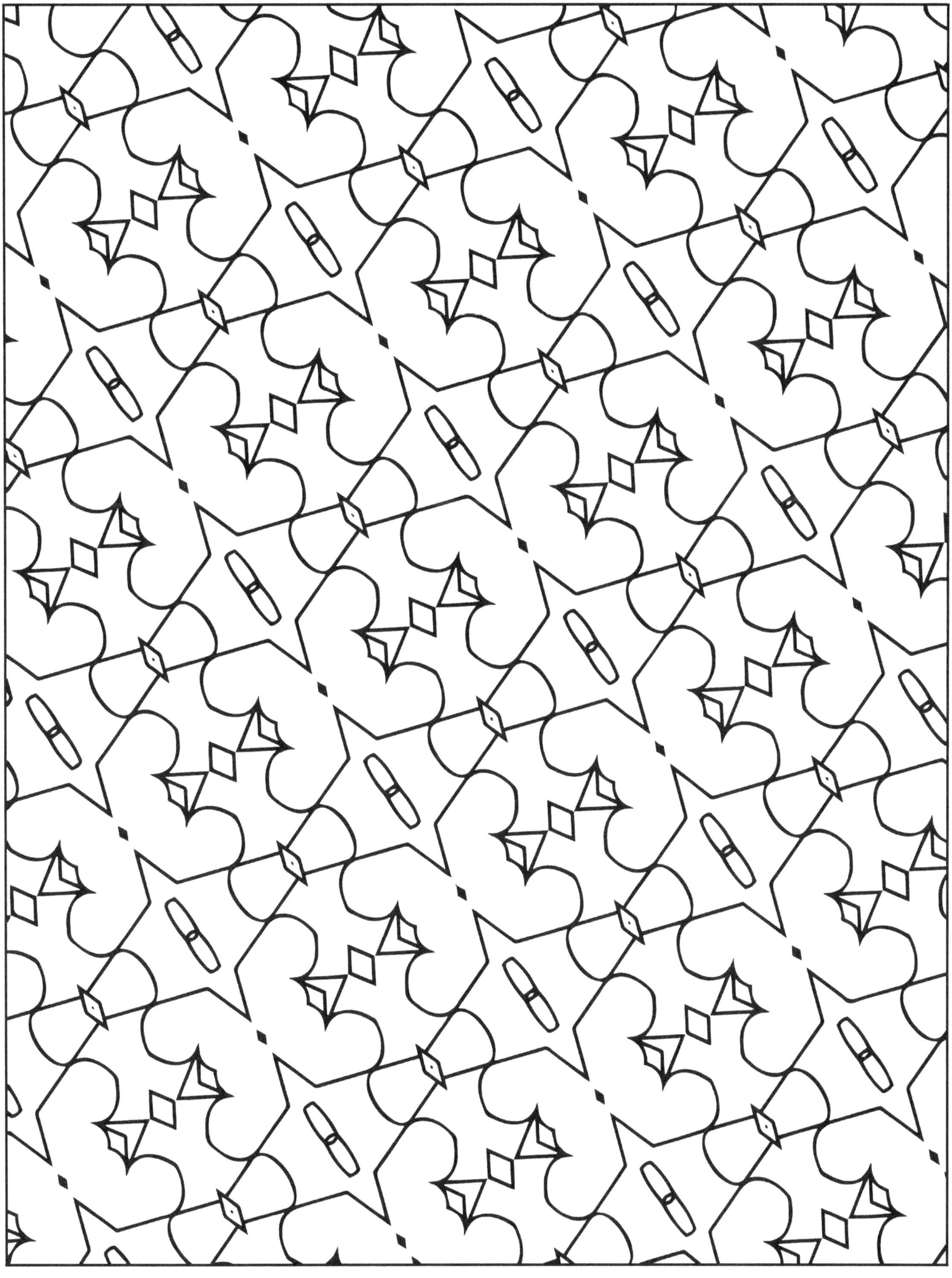

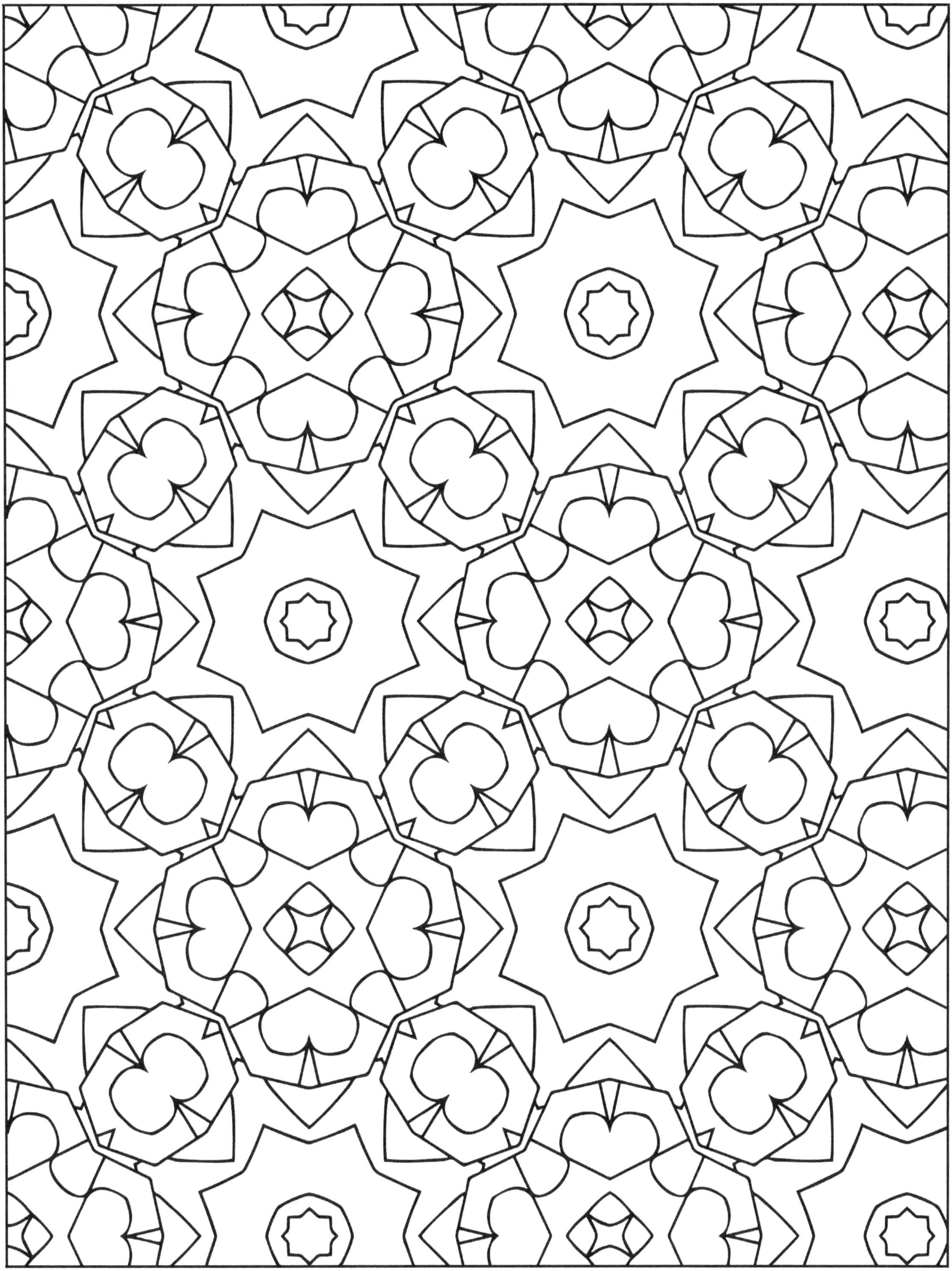

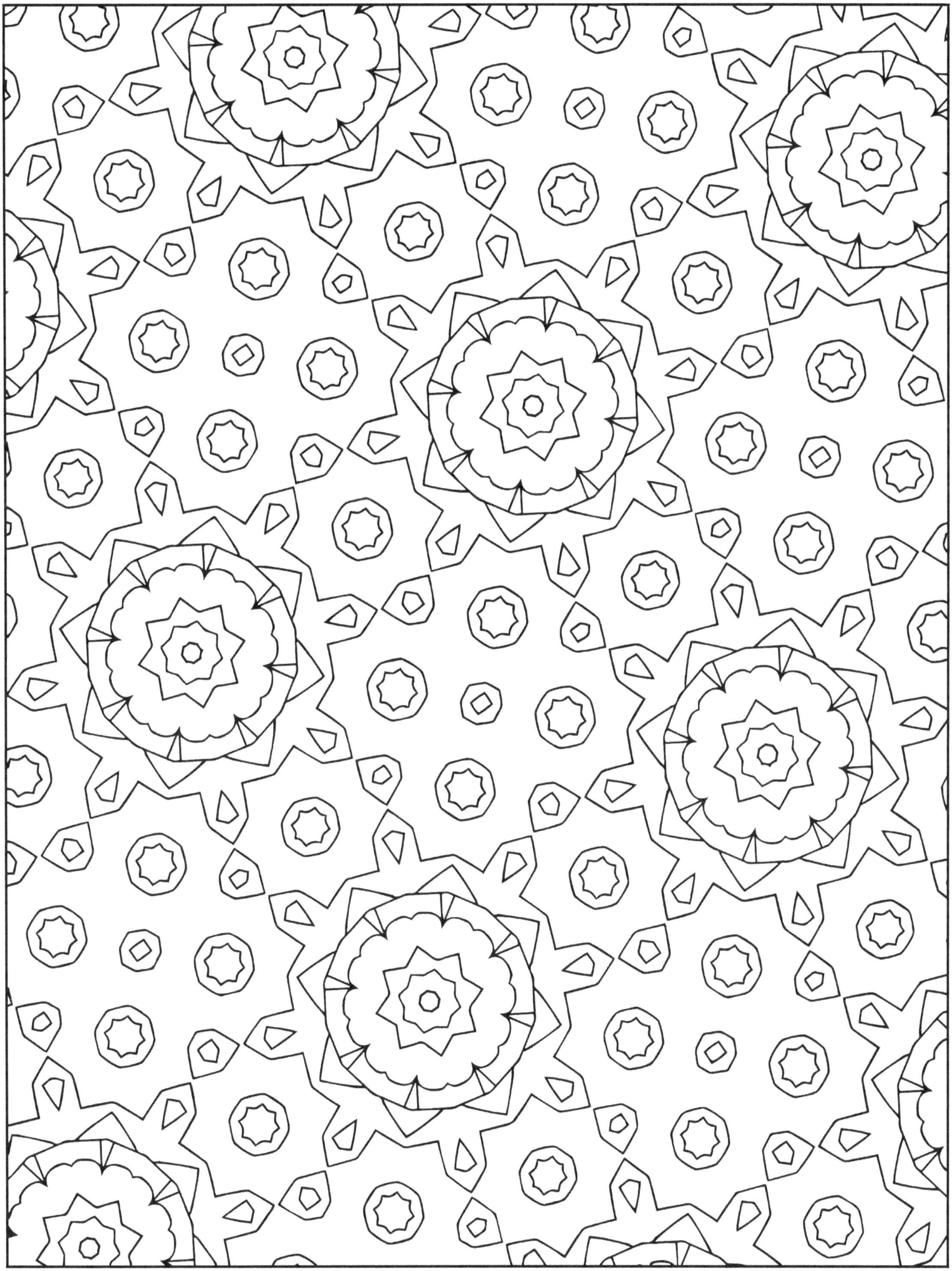

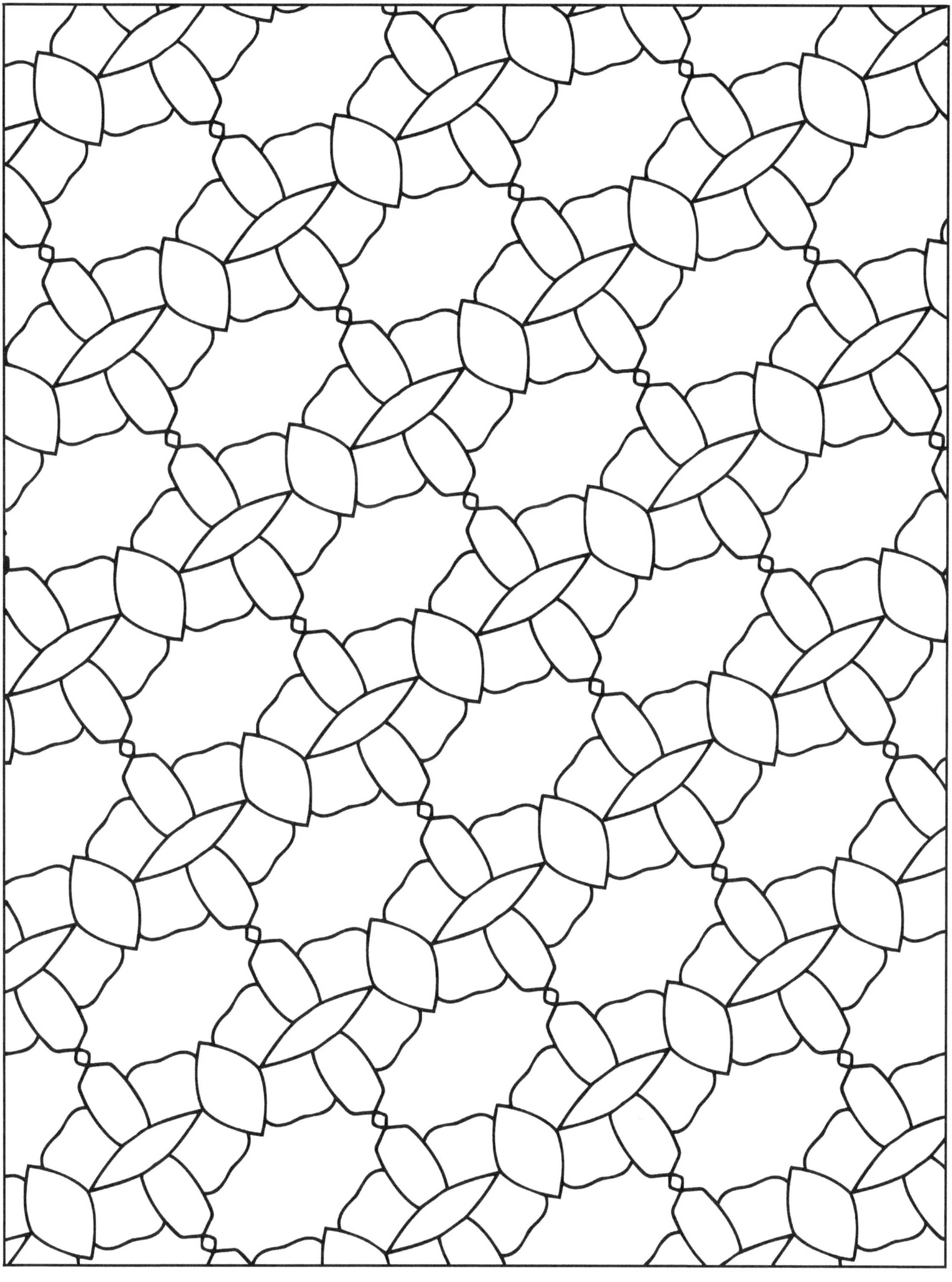

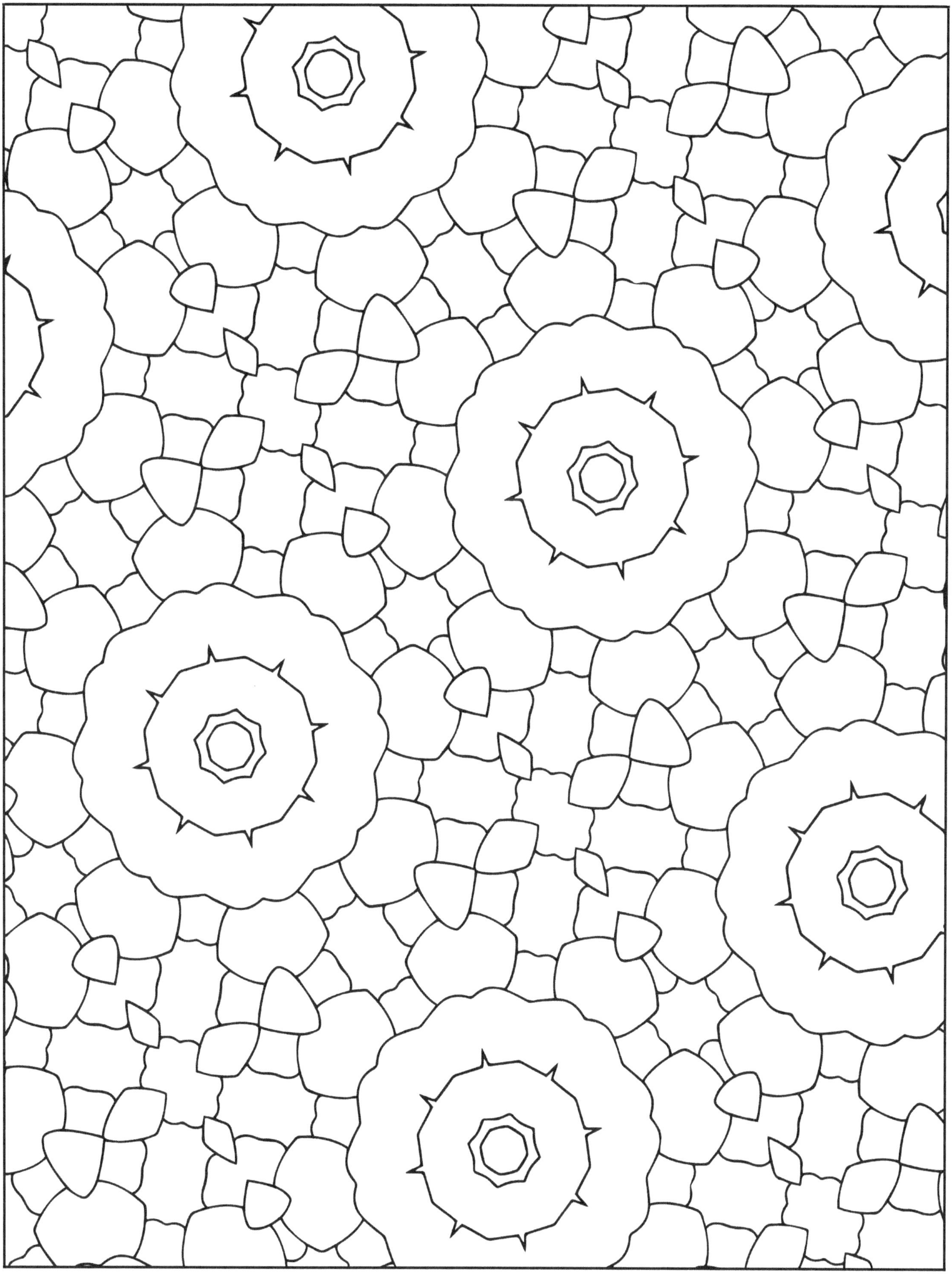

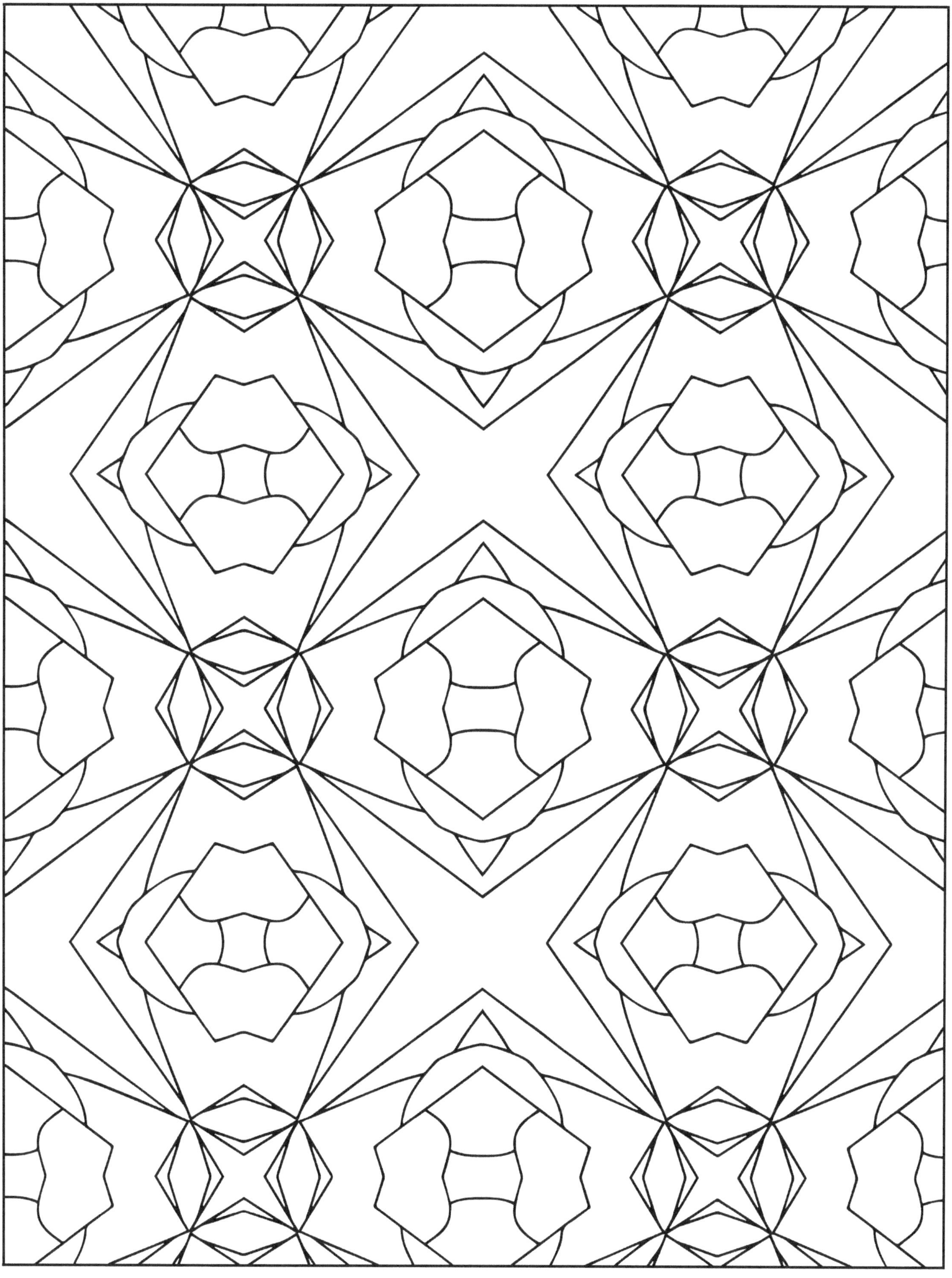

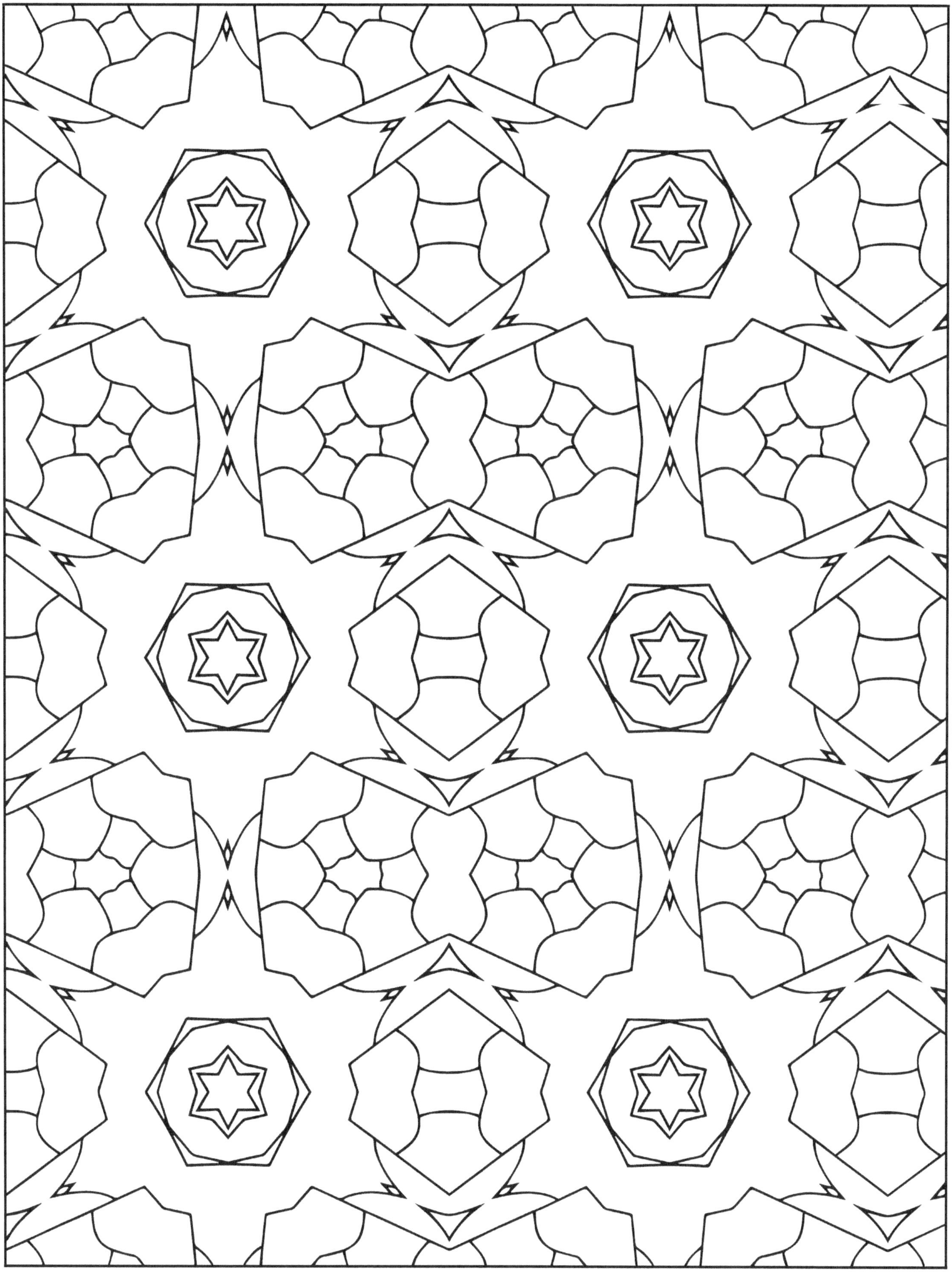

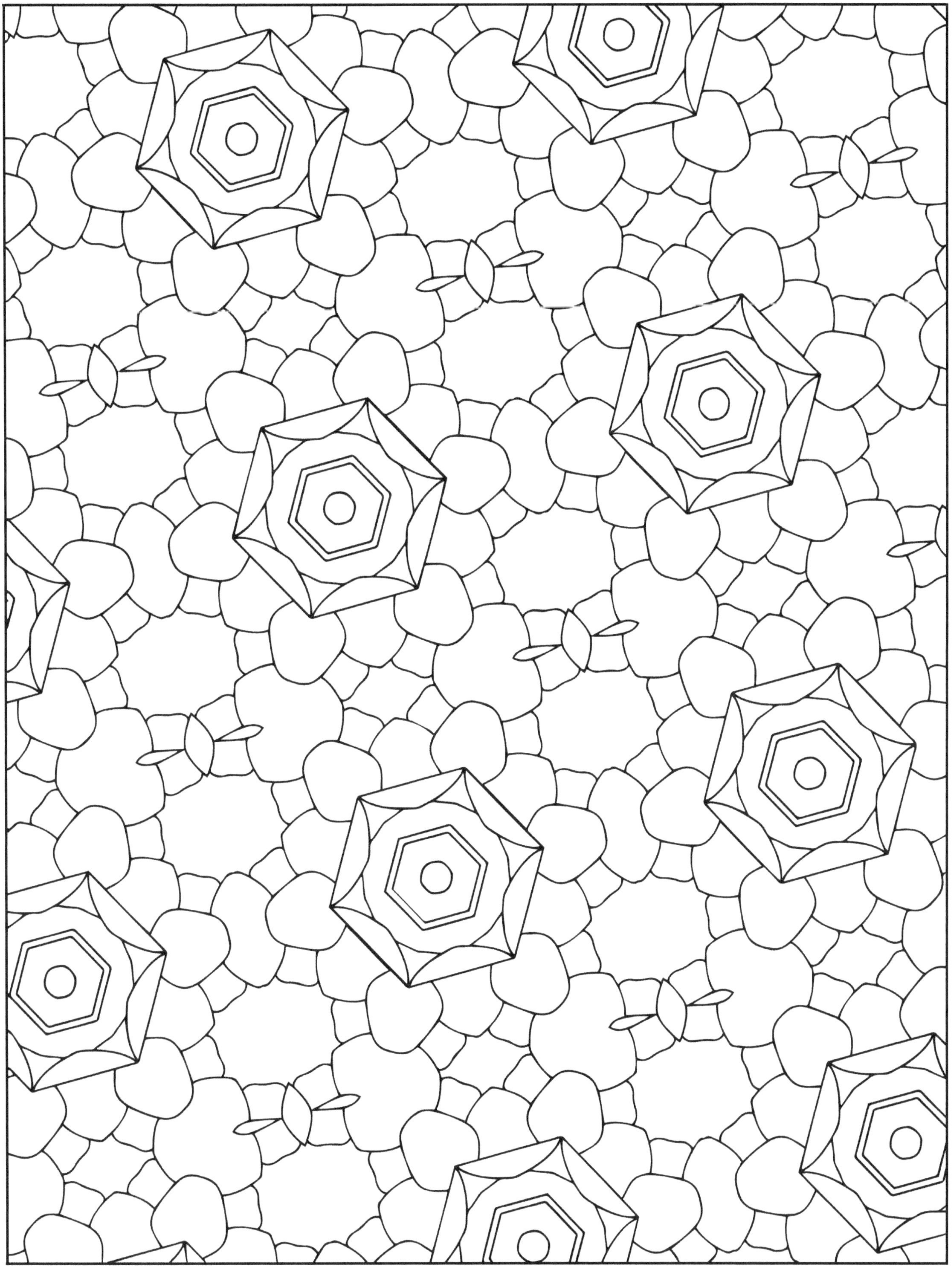

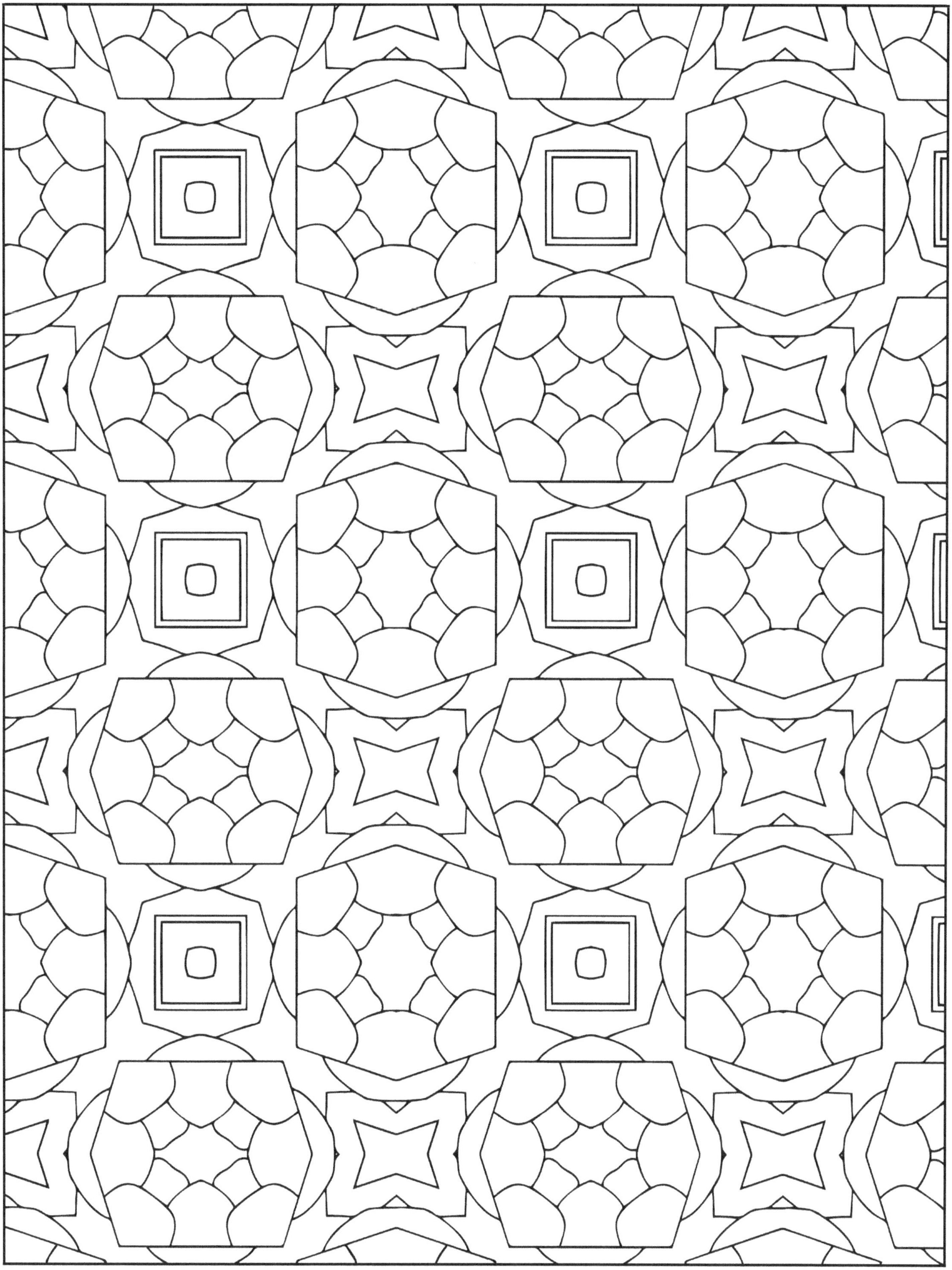

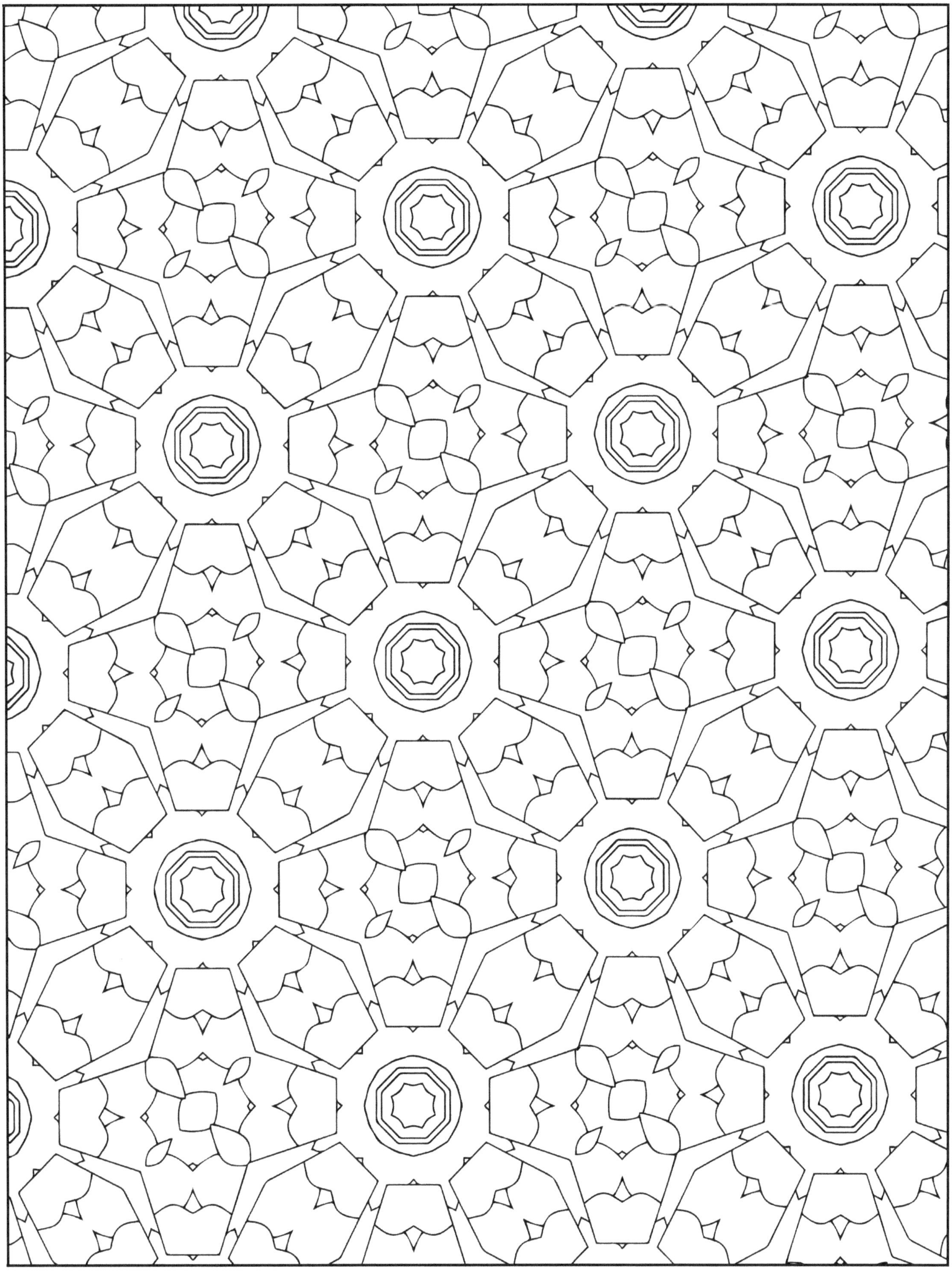

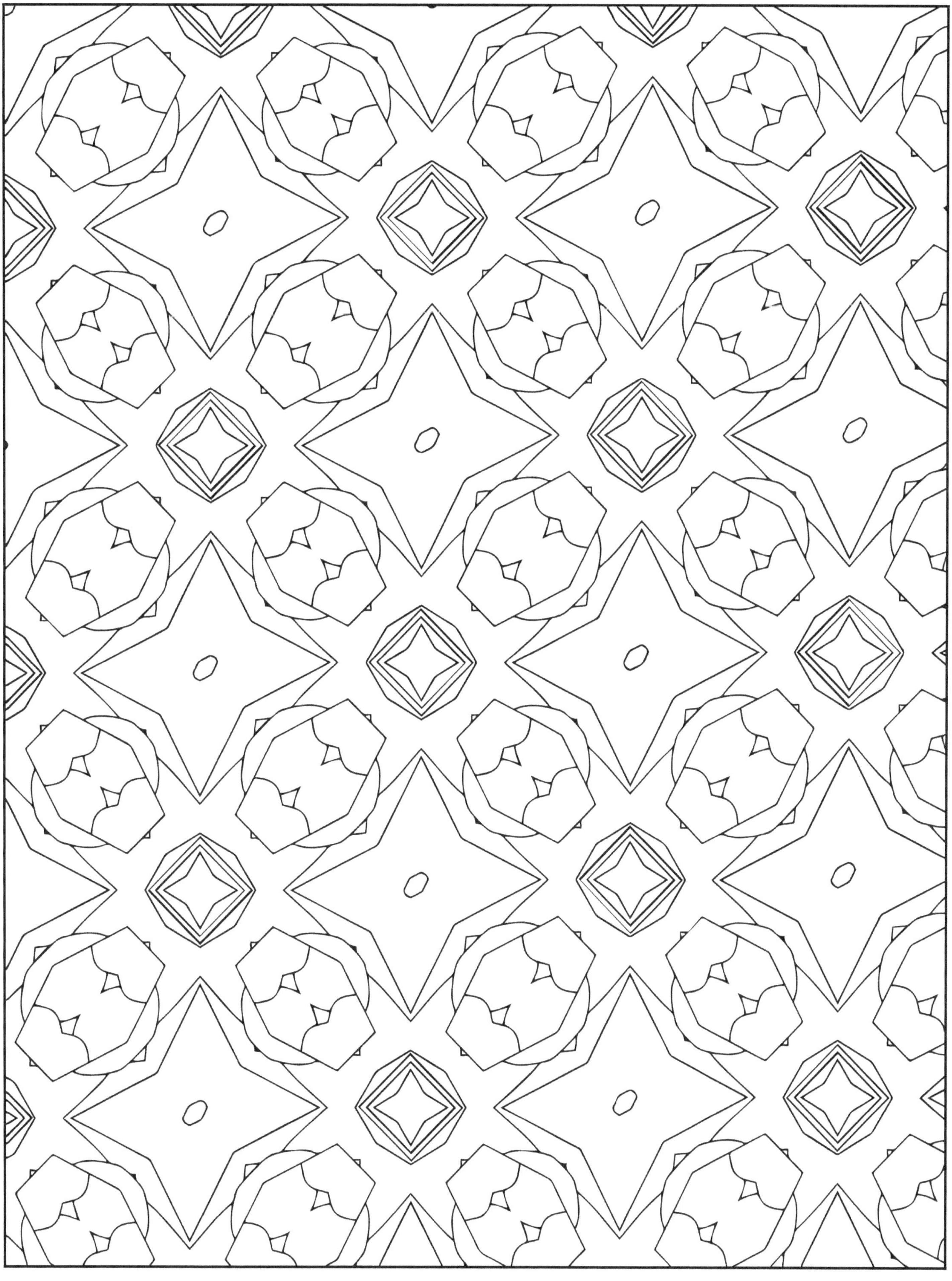

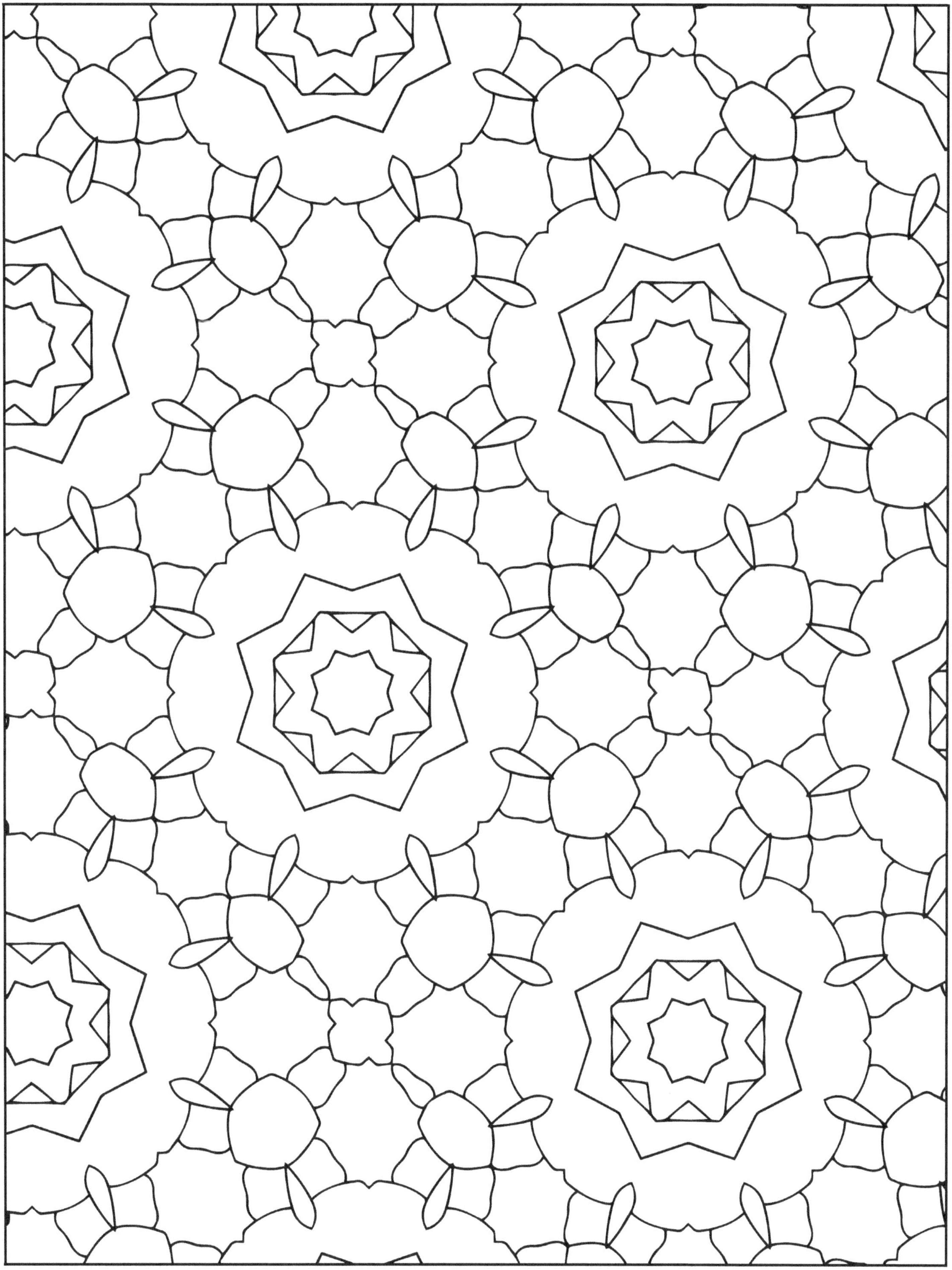

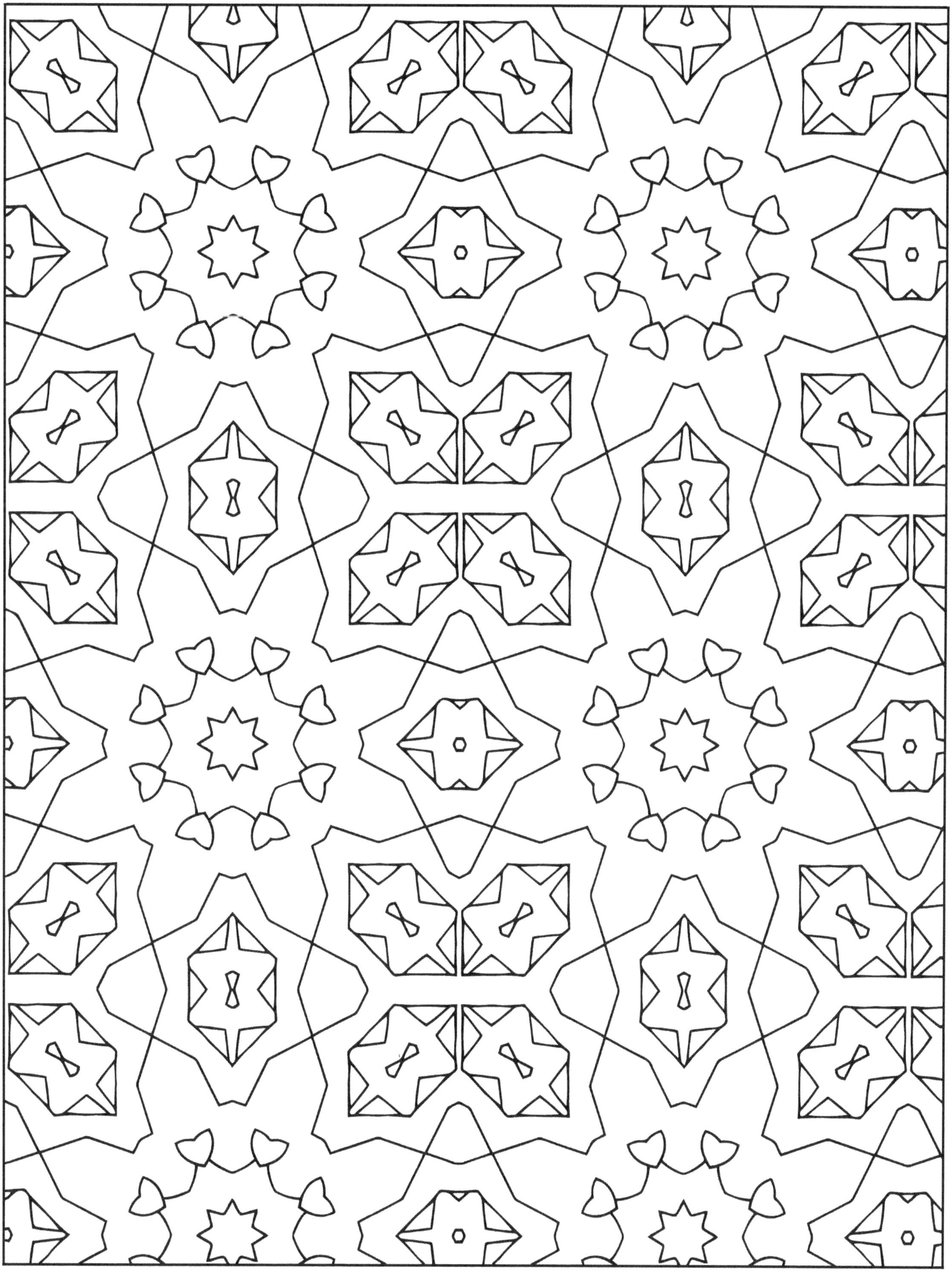

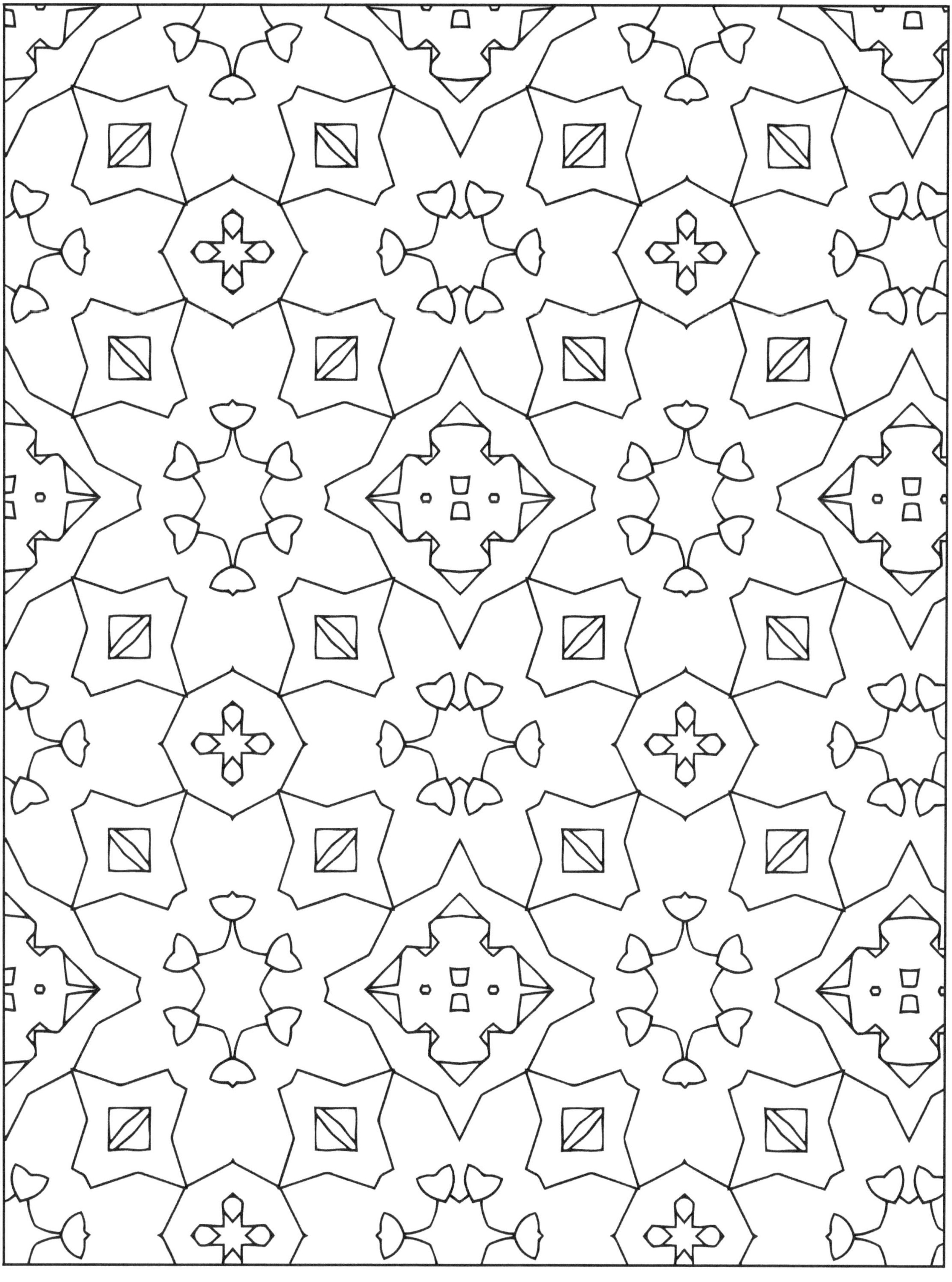

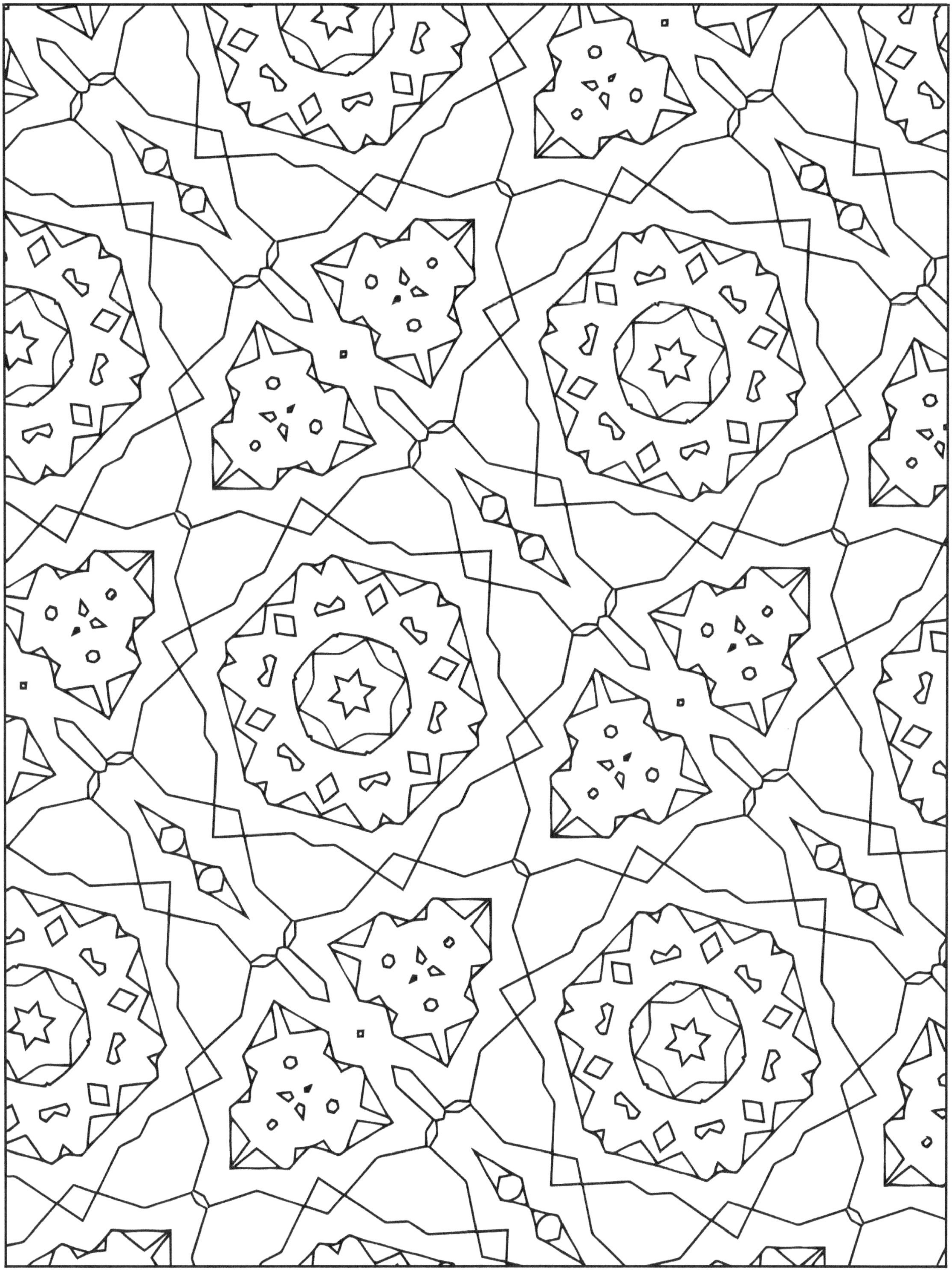

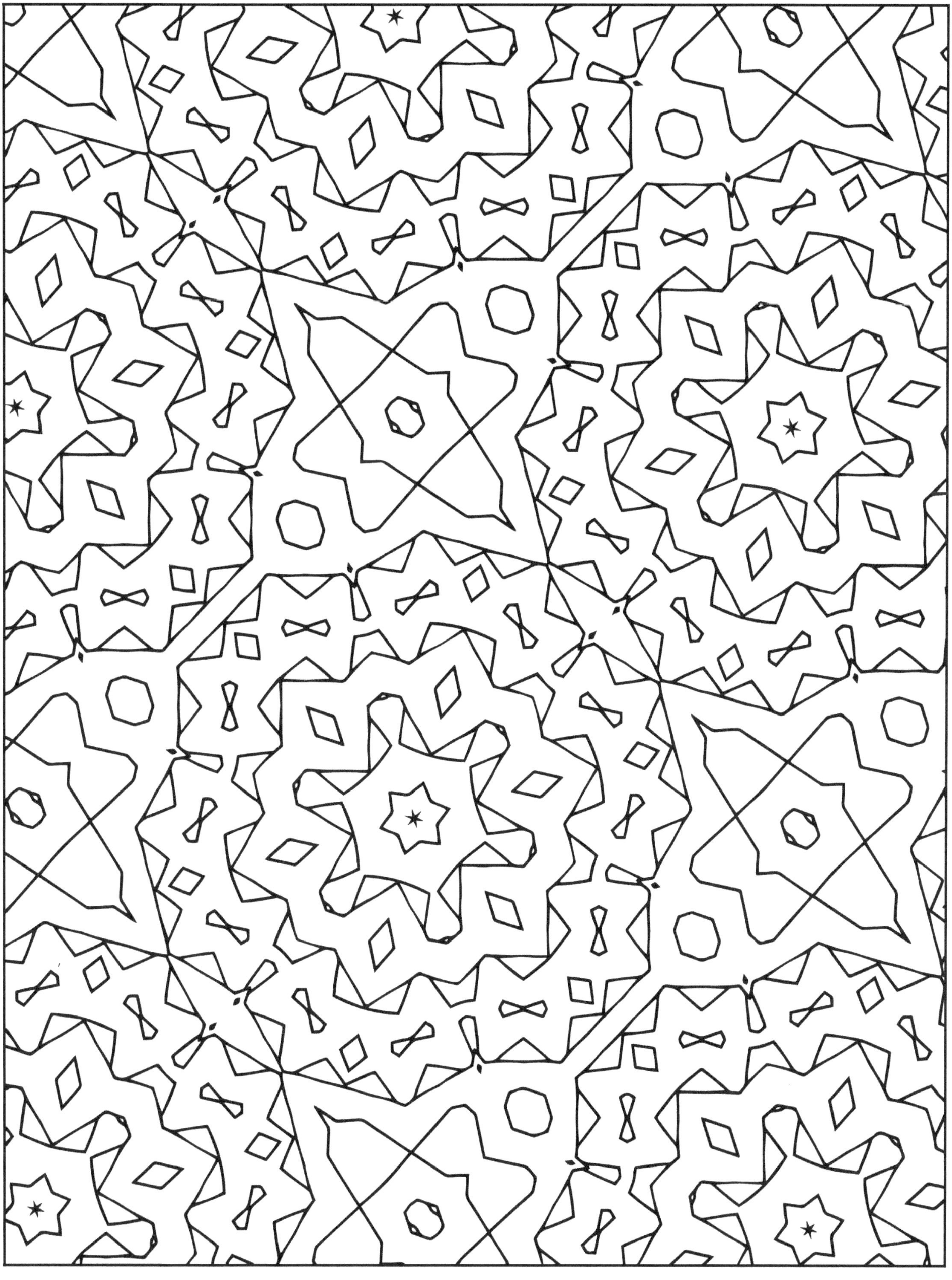

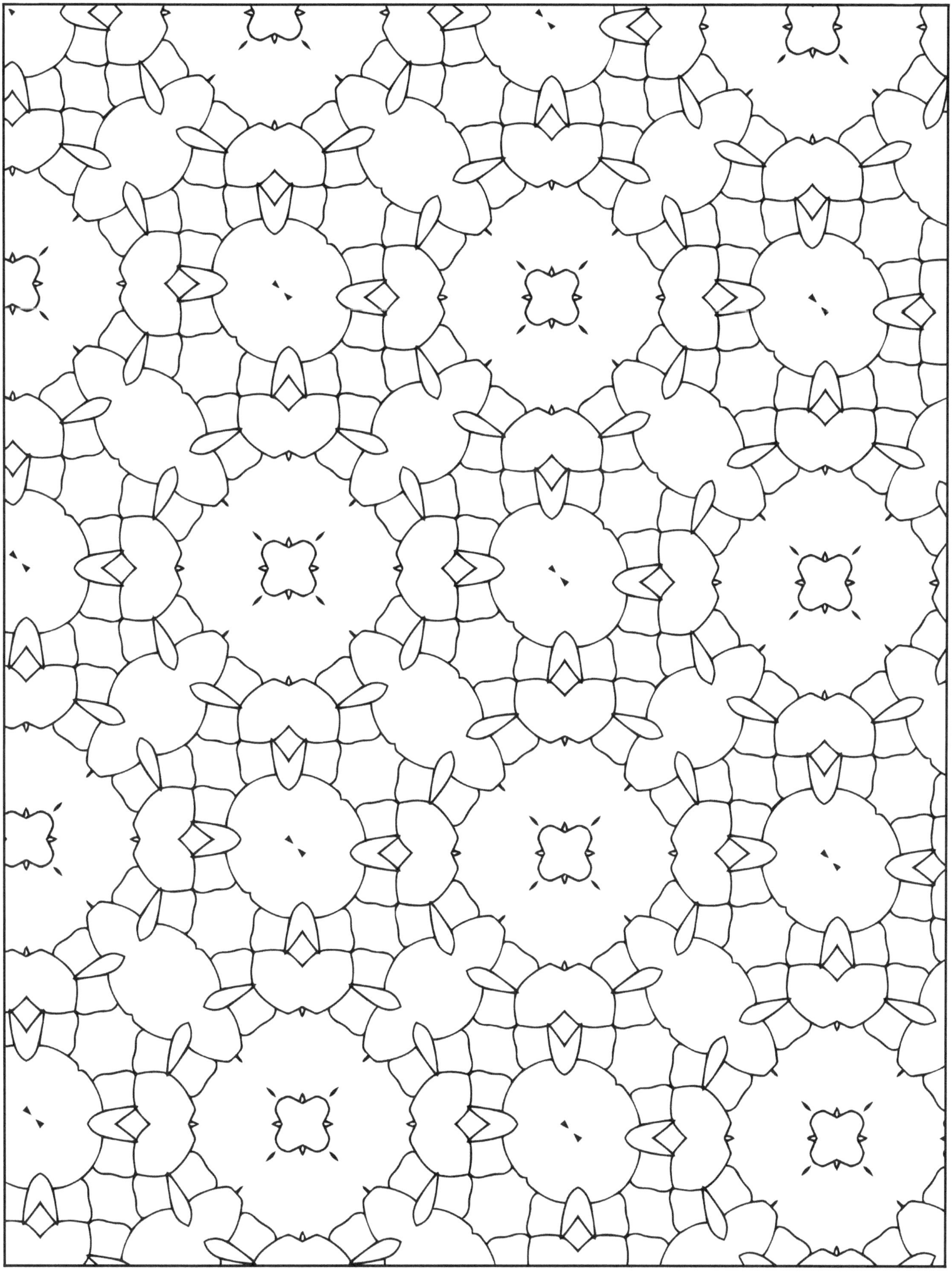

www.ingramcontent.com/pod-product-compliance
Lightning Source LLC
Chambersburg PA
CBHW081114180526
45170CB00008B/2837
9781542311373